0071498

SMITONA 99

The Technique of

NORTH AMERICAN INDIAN BEADWORK

by

MONTE SMITH

Eagle's View Publishing Company
6756 North Fork Road
Liberty, UT 84310

Library of Congress Catalog Card Number: 83-82002
ISBN 0-943604-02-8 in paperback
ISBN 0-943604-01-X in hardback

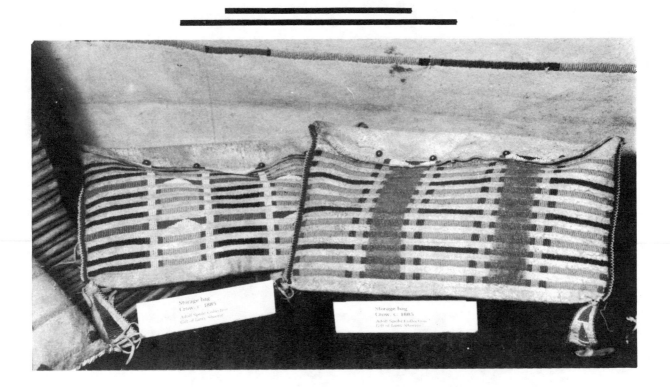

(iiA) c.1885 Storage Bags, CROW. Lazy Stitched storage bags with a brass
button closure. Note the edging on side and bottom tassles. (E)

TABLE OF CONTENTS

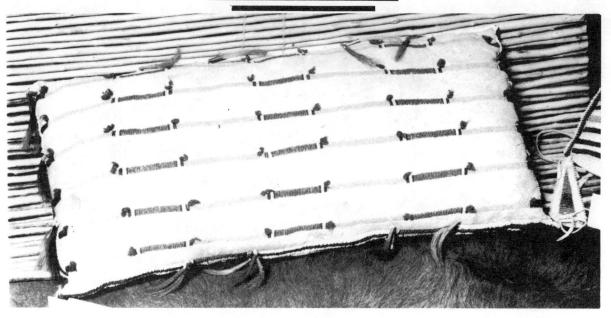

(1A) c.1890 Pillow, CHEYNNE. Lazy stitched beaded pillow with tin cones
and horsehair tassles. Made with brain-tanned buckskin. (E)

INTRODUCTION

In 1929, William C. Orchard, who is in a very real sense the "father" of every major work on North American Indian craft work since his monumental studies were completed, wrote that "With a new mode of living forced upon the Indians, the day is not far distant when distinctively aboriginal American art will be a thing of the past." Orchard cannot be faulted for not being a prophet but, in this case, he was certainly in error.

Not only has this unique American art, as but one reflection of a tenacious culture, not faded into the past, but recent history has shown a veritable explosion of interest in, and demand for,

this aboriginal craftwork. Further, some of the strength of the culture is shown in the ability to incorporate new tools (e.g., different types of beads, nylon thread, steel needles, etc.) into the craft and still maintain a product that is distinctively "Indian." You will therefore find that, contrary to what is written in many contemporary books on beadwork, "Indians" or "Native Americans" are referred to, as they should be, in the present tense throughout this text.

At the same time, just as everyone who purchases this book will not be producing the quality of bead work that will be sold at pow wows, trade fairs and rendezvous, it should not be surpr-

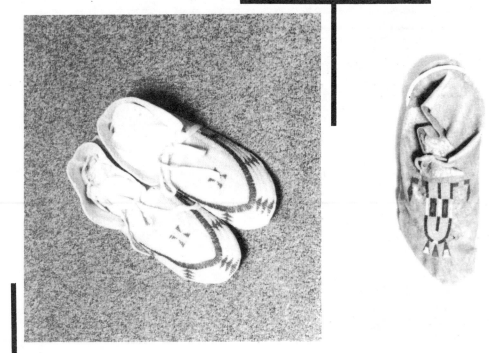

(2A) c.1895 Beaded Moccasins, CROW. Partly Beaded Moccasins made of smoked brain-tanned buckskin with rawhide soles. (E)

(2B) c.1982 Beaded Moccasins, SHOSHONI. Fully beaded, hard sole moccasins. Made by Eva McAdams from brain-tanned buckskin with yellow background. (F)

ising that not every American Indian does beadwork. Neither would you expect that every tribal member 200 years ago would be a craftsperson.

First, in years past the environment and a subsistence economy forced a division of labor in which many arts and crafts became the realm of women and were therefore considered "unmanly." The male might paint designs on tipi and shield, but the decoration of practical and ceremonial objects with quills and beads was woman's work. Also by inclination and ability, some women were better than others at decoration and it was not uncommon for creative craftspersons to devote almost all of her time possible to decoration and then trade for hides, etc., that other women had produced.

In some regards this has not changed a great deal. Whether by tradition, inclination or ability, most of the really fine beadworkers are women. It might be only natural then that most of the best books on beadwork have been written by men.

In any event, in that there are a number of good books on how to do beadwork, why write another one? Primarily because most of the books available fail to give enough information and are frustrating to the beginning beadworker. Also, because there is a continual need for more and different patterns, designs and ideas. Hopefully, this book will make a positive step at rectifying the first problem. It can be but one small contribution to the second.

(3A) Left c.1982 Beaded Moccasins, CHEYENNE. Made by Becky Elk Shoulder. Right c.1974 Beaded Moccasins, WINNEBAGO, on split elk with hard soles. (A)

(3B) c.1890 Beaded Moccasins, CHEYENNE. Fully beaded with lazy stitch technique. (E)

ACKNOWLEDGEMENTS

While only the author can be held responsible for mistakes and omissions, there are a number of people who should be acknowledged and thanked for having helped in the creation of this book. In general, this book is the result of years of preparation and much of it is the result of information received from professional beaders and instructors like Virginia Free of Winnebago as well as a multitude of excellent beaders such as the Omaha wife and daughters of Ed Snowball. These "contributors" are far too numerous to name individually but without them this book would not have been possible.

In most cases, collectors and museum people have been very helpful. Individuals who have made photographing the pictures in this book possible are: Mrs. Bessie Wardle, who made her Ute collection available; Tom Danton, curator of the Colter's Bay Museum, who took time from a very busy schedule to share the treasures from the vault; Gary Johnson, a friend whose talent ensures him immortality; the "Sunday Morning Guides" at Cody who allowed us access to their vault; Jeri Greeves of Greeves Gallery and Fort Washakie Trading Post; and, the many craftspersons who let us photograph and show their creations herein. The assistance from these people made the book much easier to complete.

In specific terms, the poem *Beading Moccasins* was contributed by Terri Meyette, Native American who is a truly gifted craftsperson. All of the illustrations were done by R. L. (*Smitty*) Smith whose talents seem to be without bounds. Michele Van Sickle not only read and re-read the manuscript but gave ideas and comments as well as providing some of the items for many of the photgraphs including the front cover. Ann Cutrubus and Brad Schroeder proof read the finished text, screamed about commas and made this a better book.

And most importantly, Nellie, who after 43 years continues to inspire and enlighten and Suzy, without whom life, in every positive aspect, would be less than it is.

•••••

PHOTO CREDITS

All photos were taken by the author. Most were taken under good conditions but a few had to be taken through glass with a resulting lack of quality; these items were important enough to add in any case.

All photos are coded as to where they were obtained. Those code numbers follow the photo description and signify that the article is from: (**A**) Eagle Feather Trading Post; (**B**) the Wardle Ute Collection; (**C**) Colter's Bay Museum; (**D**) the work of Gary Johnson; (**E**) the Museum of the Plains Indians, Cody, WY; (**F**) the Greeve's Shoshone-Arapaho Collection; (**G**) Michele Van Sickle; and, (**H**) other sources that are usually named.

(5A) c.1982 Beaded Moccasins, SHOSHONI. Eva Mc Adams beaded these on brain-tanned leather. White back ground with stripes in yellow, orange and red. Note the beaded tongues. (F)

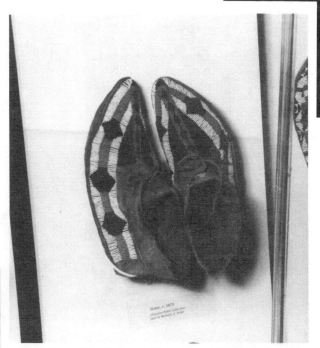

(5B) c.1875 Beaded Moccasins, SIOUX. Lazy Stitch technique moccasins from the Pohrt Collection. (E)

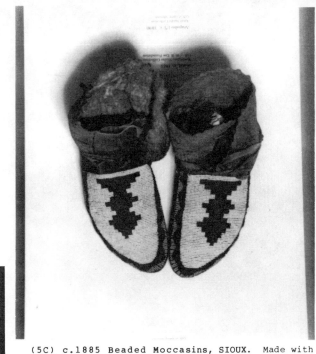

(5C) c.1885 Beaded Moccasins, SIOUX. Made with an applique running stitch, these are made of smoked brain-tanned elk. (E)

(5D) c.1915 Beaded Moccasins, CHEYENNE. An excellent example of "reservation period" lazy stitch with rawhide soles. (E)

BEADING MOCCASINS

by TERRI MEYETTE

I breathe into me
the smell of deer hide.
I send a prayer
to the hunter and
deer spirit.

I feel the soft skin
brings back memories
of elk hides
wrapped around
my body in winter.

In stillness
around and around
gifted hands go
needle sticks and
blood drops silently
into deer skin
making us one again.

The voice of wisdom
gives to me lessons
of the old ways
not spoken today.

In solitude I sit
bead the beauty
of many grandmothers
gone past.

Respect comes
when I look
upon the beauty complete

Love shine's radiant
when I give them away
My heart smiles.

Sitting cross legged
on my woven blanket
I burn herbs purifying
the space.
In silence the making
of moccasin begins.

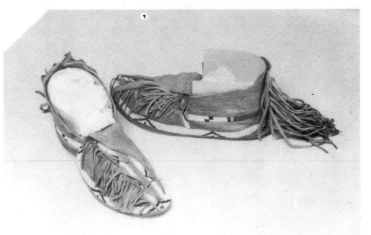

(6A) c.1875 Beaded Moccasins, ARAPAHO(Southern).
Excellent, typical example with 14 cm. heel fringe.
Measure 26.5 x 9 cm. each. White, Dk Blue and Red. (C)

6

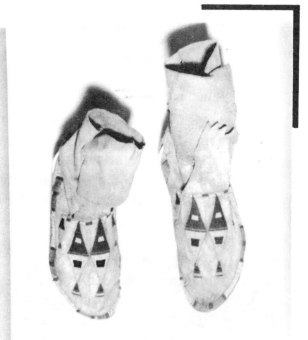

(7A) c.1885 Beaded Moccasins, SAC & FOX. Excellent applique example that combines geometric with floral designs. (E)

(7B) c.1890 Beaded Moccasins, CROW. This partial beaded pair come above the ankle. Made of brain-tan leather. (E).

(7C) c.1982 Contemporary Rosettes, SHOSHONE AND ARAPAHO. Some good examples of present day work. Note the different styles of necklaces. (F)

The purpose of this book is not to provide a comprehensive history of beads, but it is useful to know when different kinds of beads were used in North America. In general terms there are four (4) different periods of the types of beads used:

(1) The Pre-Columbian bead work period with extensive use of shell, pearl, bone, stone and metal beads; (2) the pre-embroidery or bead necklace period with the use of trade, crow and other relatively large beads; (3) the Pony or "Real" bead period that saw a pronounced increase in the use of beads for decoration and a corresponding decrease in the aboriginal art of porcupine quillwork; and (4) the seed bead or contemporary bead period.

It is important to remember that the dates of these respective periods are only exact as to when they began. For instance, it is known that *Period Two* started in 1492 but did not gain prominance until the 1700s in the East and the 1800s west of the Mississippi. However, just because a new type of bead was introduced it does not mean that the old ones were no longer used. Even today the Navajos are using "ghost beads" that were prominent in *Period One* and many tribes are using Pony Beads from *Period Three*.

(8A) c.1982 Moccasins, PIAUTE. Contemporary moccasins made by the Earl Pikyavit family on brain-tanned buckskin. (A)

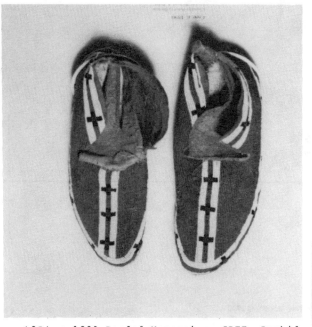

(8B) c.1890 Beaded Moccasins, CREE. Rawhide soles. Note the straight and even beaded rows and the distinctive style of tongue. (E)

To some extent, the introduction of beads to various tribes corresponds with the advent of the fur traders. Beads, though fairly heavy, were commonly used by traders as a medium exchange for furs; so much so that in the early nineteenth century the Northwest Company paid part of their employees' wages in beads. Still, this is not always a good guide as, for instance, the Onate expedition to New Mexico, at the end of the 16th century, carried over 80,000 glass beads of various kinds with them for trading and gifts, and some types of small "seed" beads present in North America by 1500 have remained virtually unchanged to the present time.

Still, Europeans in search of furs had much to do with the introduction of new kinds of beads to Native Americans. The French, and to a much more limited extent the English, used beads as gifts, and missionaries used beads in their quest for converts to Christiantiy. But traders were the main source of glass beads.

In 1760 a beaver skin could be traded for a six foot string of beads. By 1807, however, supply and demand had brought the price down to two pounds of beads for one beaver skin (in this same time period a trade gun cost ten beaver skins). White was the most common color of beads used and tariff lists from the early 19th century show that 562 distinct types of beads were being imported.

It cannot, therefore, be overstressed that if the craftsperson is concerned with the replication of early Indian work, it is going to require much research and study to do so. A war shirt, for instance,

(9A) c.1890 Beaded Moccasins, SIOUX. Fully beaded, smoked brain-tanned moccasins with horsehair and tin cones tassles on the toungues. (E)

(9B) c.1890 Beaded Moccasins, COMMANCHE. These excellent moccasins have tin cones attached to the vamp fringe on toes and extra long heel fringe said to be used to cover tracks. (E)

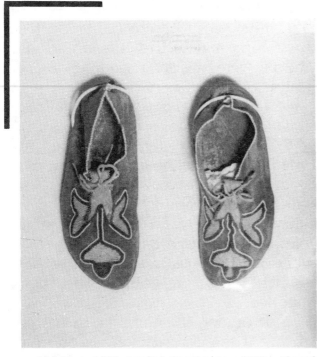

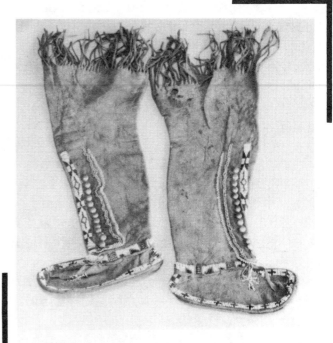

(10A) c.1885 Beaded Moccasins, OTTO. Floral design moccasins. Note the edging around the tongue and uppers on this pair. (E)

(10B) c.1875 Child's Boot Moccasins, KIOWA. Hardsole, beaded buckskin moccasins with attached leggings and flap with german silver buttons. (C)

(10C) c.1915 Beaded Moccasins, CREE. Fully beaded moccasins with white background. Note the fine craftsmanship and attractive flow of the design. (E)

(10D) c.1890 Beaded Moccasins, SHOSHONE. Fully beaded toe moccasins with unusual style of bars down the toe. (E)

that is suppose to reflect what a Blackfoot man wore in 1780 would probably not have seed beads on it. On the other hand, if you are primarily interested in a beautiful finished product, go to the Browning Pow Wow and copy any one of the outstanding war shirts in evidence today. You will not only find seed beads, but nymo thread; you will also find a reflection of strength and honor. Either perspective has its merits but the creation of *Authentic Traditional* craftwork is the more difficult of the two.

•••••

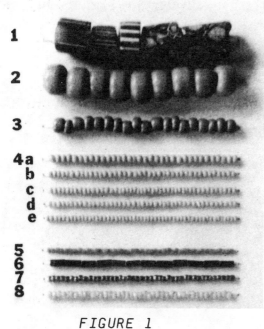

FIGURE 1

Shown are (1) Trade Beads, (2) Crow Beads, (3) Pony Beads and (4) Seed Beads: (a) 10/°, (b) 11/°, (c) 12/°, (d) 13/° and (e) 14/°; (5) 15/° Hexigons, (6) #2 Bugle Beads, (7) 12/° 3 Cut Beads and (8) 11/° Japanese Cut Beads.

Figure One pictures some of the beads that were accessible in the past along with some that are very popular in contemporary times; all may be purchased today. Trade and Crow beads are the largest, Pony beads are smaller and seed beads smaller still. Seed beads are numbered 9/° thru 14/°, etc., and a general rule is that **the larger the number the smaller the bead**. Therefore, a size 12/° seed bead is smaller than a size 10/°.

Beads that were first introduced into this country came from Italy and what is now Czechoslovakia. The Czech trade grew over time and today only a very small percentage of imported beads are Venetian.

Another growing source of glass seed beads is Japan, but at this time, with the exception of the 11/° cut bead, their product continues to be uneven and therefore difficult to work with.

When beads are imported they come in kilos (*approximately 2.2 pounds*) and many are on strings. Strung kilos are divided into bunches called "hanks" that have between 20 and 24 strings, usually 10 inches long. In that beads are imported by weight, the number of hanks in each kilo varies with the size of the beads. For instance, a kilo of size 10/° beads will have about 19 hanks, whereas there are approximately 28 hanks in a kilo of size 12/° seed beads. There are more beads, regardless of whether they are on strings or in bulk, in a kilo of size 12/° beads and they usually cost more.

BEAD SELECTION

One of the most important secrets in beading is the **selection of beads**, and a good part of this selection can be made when the beads are purchased. First, as indicated above, the most uniform beads are sold in hanks and on strings. However, most craft supply stores sell seed beads in plastic containers or bags and this means that, when buying beads that are packaged, you have to examine them to make sure that they are all relatively uniform in shape and size. When buying beads that are strung, hold the string horizontally so that the beads touch, but are not crowded, and check for uniformity. If the string is held vertically with the beads resting on each other it is possible to gauge the outside dimensions but not the size of the holes. In either case, you are interested in how the beads match both on the outside and the inside. If the package or hanks have 90% or better of the beads that are uniform they are good beads to work with.

Then, as strange as this seems, after all of the bead colors have been chosen in the same size (say size 11/⁰ for instance) place all of the colors next to each other and make sure they are all the same size! It is not uncommon to find that different colors within the same bead size will vary in dimension. Moreover, size will vary from dye batch to dye batch so that single color might have a size difference from batch to batch. Ideally all colors that are the same bead size will have the same dimensions; if

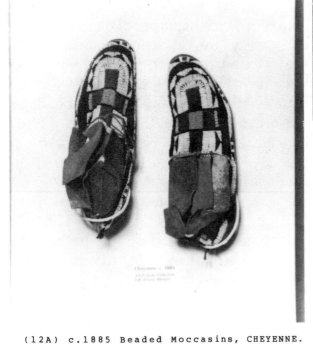

(12A) c.1885 Beaded Moccasins, CHEYENNE. Attractive geometric design with rawhide soles. (E)

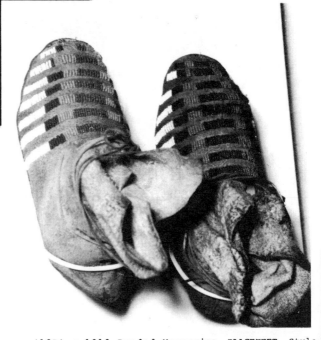

(12B) c.1910 Beaded Moccasins, BLACKFEET. Style is very traditional and done on smoked brain-tanned elk hide. (E)

that is not possible there are techniques described later in this book to overcome the problem but beading will be easier if you have uniform beads to begin with.

How many beads should you buy? Just like gasoline . . . more than you need. One hank or ounce of 10/^{O} beads will cover about 12 square inches but that kind of figure is not much help unless all of the beading is going to be in one color. The problem is that beads will vary not only slightly in size but also in hue and shade from dye batch to dye batch. So if you purchase a hank of color #324 (Sky Blue) and run out before the project is finished there is a very good chance that you might not be able to match the beads you have been using. Therefore, it is a good idea to buy more beads than needed. Further, almost any reputable dealer will trade for other beads if you end up with

too many beads of a particular color when the project is finished. (Be sure and save some for any repairs that might have to be made later.)

However, if an authentic looking project from 1885 is attempted, forget all of the above. Beads were very uneven in those days and conditions forced using what was on hand, but it takes a good beadworker to manage this kind of craft.

A final word on beads and beginnings: Most people who are just starting feel more comfortable with a size 10/^{O} or 11/^{O} seed bead because of the larger size and for a number of reasons this makes sense. The size makes it possible to cover an area faster for a feeling of accomplishment, it is easier to thread the needle, it is easier to gauge uniformity in the larger beads, etc. The Scout leader who starts his beading class with 13/^{O} beads is really

(13A) Left c.1875 Beaded Moccasins, SIOUX. Two piece, hardsole, buckskin moccasin with large forged tongue. Sewn with sinew. Right c.1880 Moccasins, FLATHEAD. One piece, softsole, buckskin. (C)

(13B) c.1890 Beaded Bag, FLATHEAD. Great example of applique running stitch using 10/^{O} size beads. Has a medium blue background. (E)

flirting with disaster if not with death.

MATERIALS

It is a very good idea to have a suitable container for all of your bead-work supplies. Craft or artist boxes are available or they may be home-made. In any event, a container is needed that will hold thread, bees wax, needles, scissors, pliers and beads.

FIGURE TWO

Figure Two is a good example of such a bead box, in that it has a couple of trays that have compartments as well as an area in the bottom for larger items and extra materials.

Unless sinew is going to be used in beading (described in the Chapter on Sewn Beadwork), you will need needles and thread. It is easy to purchase the proper needle with the following information in mind.

Beading requires the use of needles made specifically for that purpose and come in two main classes: **Beading**, or

(14A) c.1880 Moccasins, WINNEBAGO. One piece, softsole with puckered seam up front. Has attached cuff. Right c.1885 Moccasins, POTAWATOMI. Abstract floral patterns in earth tones. (C)

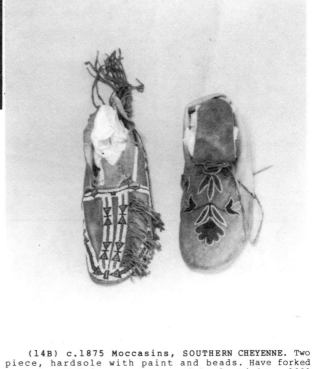

(14B) c.1875 Moccasins, SOUTHERN CHEYENNE. Two piece, hardsole with paint and beads. Have forked tongue and fringe on vamp and heel. Right c.1880 Moccasins, SANTEE SIOUX. Two piece, hardsole mocs (C)

14

long beading needles and **Sharps** ,or short beading needles.

The Figure on the right shows a number 12 needle in Beading and Sharps. As with beads, the bigger the number the smaller around the needle, and as long as English needles are used the number corresponds to the bead size. In other words, a number ten (10) needle can be used with 10/^{O} beads. However, it is good practice to use a needle that is smaller than the beads as many times the thread has to go through the bead a number of times. Therefore, if a size 11/^{O} bead is used it is probably good to use a number 12 needle. At the same time, the smaller the needle the easier it is to break, so it would not be a good idea to use a 15 needle unless you were using 13/^{O} beads. The kind of needle used depends upon the work, and as a general rule "Beading" or long needles are used for loom work and "Sharps" or short needles are used for sewn beadwork.

However, the description given above applies only to beading needles made in England. These needles tend to be made of fine steel and to be more sturdy than others that are imported. On the other hand, Japanese needles tend to be more flexible (with more "give"). It should also be noted that Japanese needles are numbered differently: whereas English needles may be obtained in numbers 10, 11, 12, 13 and 15 (these relate to bead sizes), Japanese needles come in

(15A) c.1885 Women's Leggings, CHEYENNE. Beaded and painted buckskin leggings with fringe and sewn with sinew. Measurements are 47 x 19 cm. (C)

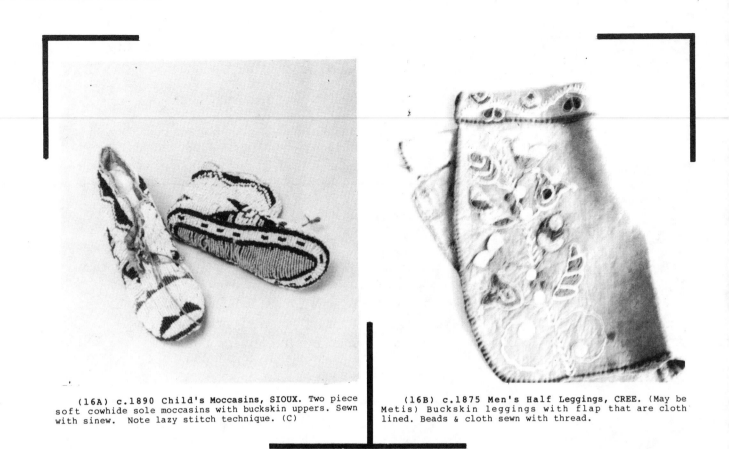

(16A) c.1890 Child's Moccasins, SIOUX. Two piece soft cowhide sole moccasins with buckskin uppers. Sewn with sinew. Note lazy stitch technique. (C)

(16B) c.1875 Men's Half Leggings, CREE. (May be Metis) Buckskin leggings with flap that are cloth lined. Beads & cloth sewn with thread.

numbers 14 and 16 that correspond to beads and English needles 10 and 12 respectively.

Whether English or Japanese needles are used depends completely on personal preference and it is a good idea to try both to decide which will work best for your style of work.

The thread that is used more than any other is "nymo" or nylon and in this case **the larger the letter, the larger the thread.** Size 00, 0 or A is the finest thread. It also comes in sizes B, D and F, with F being the largest and used mostly for stringing. The size thread used depends upon the size bead and needle. For instance, if you are using size 13/º beads and a number 15 English beading needle you would use size A nymo, or if

you are using a size 11/º bead and a number 14 Japanese needle you could use size D nymo. The larger the thread, the stronger it is. The best selling threads are sizes D and A.

The following chart will act as a guide for beginning. However, this is a general outline and other combinations will work:

	Needles		Nymo
Beads	_English_	_Japanese_	_Thread_
10/º	10 or 11	14	D
11/º	11 or 12	14	D
12/º	12 or 13	16	A or B
13/º	13 or 15		A

Nymo is excellent for beading in that it is extremely strong. It will, however, stretch and this can be either a

16

benefit or liability depending upon the kind of beading being done. For instance, if a belt is being loom beaded that will go around the waist or an overlaid stitch on leather apparel that will stretch with use, nymo is excellent in that it will stretch to some extent with the article it is sewn to. On the other hand, if the project will not tolerate any give at all, it might be better to use cotton or quilting thread.

Another product that works well is called "**imitation sinew**." This is actually a number of nylon threads that have been wound together and impregnated with bees wax. The imitation sinew can be split down to the size you need or used as is for stringing or leather sewing.

Regardless of the kind of thread used, you will want to use bees wax on it. Waxing the thread will accomplish two things: (1) it tends to make the thread stronger and (2) it will eliminate tangles and knots in the thread. For best results enough wax is used to eliminate tangles but not so much that it comes off when the thread is pulled through the beads. Also, when bugle beads and 15/O hexigon beads are used the wax will prevent the thread from being cut by the edges of these types of beads.

Again, this will be a matter of personal taste, but it is usually an advantage to start with a thread about 24 inches long. One aid in threading the needle is to make a good clean cut at an angle before waxing the thread. Then use a small amount of bees wax to make

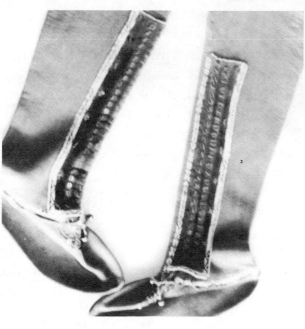

(17A) c.1880 Women's Boots, COMMANCHE. Hardsoled moccasins with buckskin upper and high, fringed top. Extra flap added to top. 60 cm. high. (C)

(17B) c.1895 Beaded Dress, SIOUX. Lazy stitched, geometric design on brain-tanned buckskin dress. Basic background of medium blue. (E)

(18A & B) c.1955 Fully Beaded Women's Purses,
UTE. Beautiful examples of applique "running stitch"
done on the Ft. Duchesne Reservation, Utah. (B)

a good sharp point and run it through the eye of the needle; *needle threaders* are also available at most craft stores.

When doing bead work it is best to have a large flat area that is covered with a dish towel or desk blotter. Unless you enjoy eye strain, be sure there is adequate light.

The way the beads are separated for use will depend upon personal preference. Experiment with any of the following to see what works best, but remember that the main objective is to be able to select uniform beads as the beading is done. Some beadworkers simply place all of their beads in one shallow saucer and select the beads they want to use out of it. Others will have a number of small, shallow saucers (white

is probably the best color) with different colors in each one. Still other crafts-persons simply make small piles of beads of different colors on the cloth and select from them. Another method is to select the bead directly from the string they come on; this allows you to see which beads are uniform, to bring the beads to you when the beading thread is short and to insure that two strings will go through the hole in the beads chosen. Any of these methods, or others, will work and trying different methods will help find which works best for you.

After you have started stringing the beads on the thread it may be that, even with the greatest of care in selection, there are times when you find that there are too many beads on a thread, or that an irregular bead has been strung. Sometimes it is easier to break the bead than take off all of the beads behind it. Breaking a bead is always a bit risky as the beads are glass and they may cut the thread. In order to minimize the risk (as shown in *Figure 5*) the bead should be broken with a pair of needlenose pliers by squeezing it from the side. Never crush the bead by placing it within the jaws of the pliers and squeezing them over the thread or it is probable that the thread will be cut.

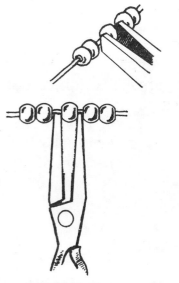

FIGURE 5

PERSPECTIVE

One thing to remember about beading that will save a lot of frustration is that **the project is always beaded before putting it together.** It is much more difficult to bead moccasins that have been sewn together, and even doing

(19B) c.1905 Women's Purse, NORTHERN PLAINS. Applique beaded purse with typical geometric designs. Beaded to smoked, brain-tanned buckskin. Note two styles of edging used. (E)

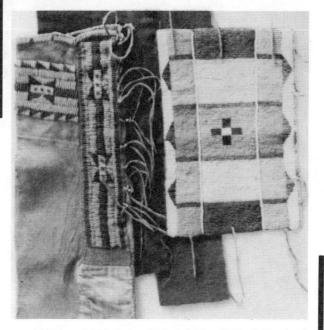

(19A) c.1885 Women's Leggings, CROW. Fully beaded buckskin leggings with thong ties; sewn to red trade cloth. Sewn with sinew. (E)

a war shirt is more difficult once the pieces have been stitched in place.

Also, you should remember what could be called "beading perspective." **A beaded article is viewed and appreciated for the overall effect and not for the small imperfections that are in it**. This does not mean that the work can be sloppy or haphazard as that will show through; it does mean that most of the time the small errors or irregularities that are almost a certainty in beading will never be noticed by anyone but the beadworker who made the item. Of course, as the art is perfected and skills acquired, these "mistakes" become fewer, but it is difficult to do away with them completely. If justification is needed for this it is good to remember one of the beliefs of the Winnebago Nation: *Only Earth Maker can create anything perfect*. Many times you will see a piece of Winnebago beadwork that is excellent and find that somewhere in the work there is a bead of a different color that just does not belong there. This is simply the craftperson's admission of his or her imperfection.

If ever you have a critic examine your beadwork who has the audacity to point out a small error, simply tell them that only Earth Maker can create anything perfect.

(20A) c.1900 Fully Beaded Vest, UMATILLA or YAKIMA. Beaded velveteen vest with back tie and lined with black cloth. NOTE applique technique. (C)

(20B) c.1880 Fully Beaded Vest, SIOUX. Man's vest of buckskin and beaded with sinew. NOTE lazy stitch technique. (C)

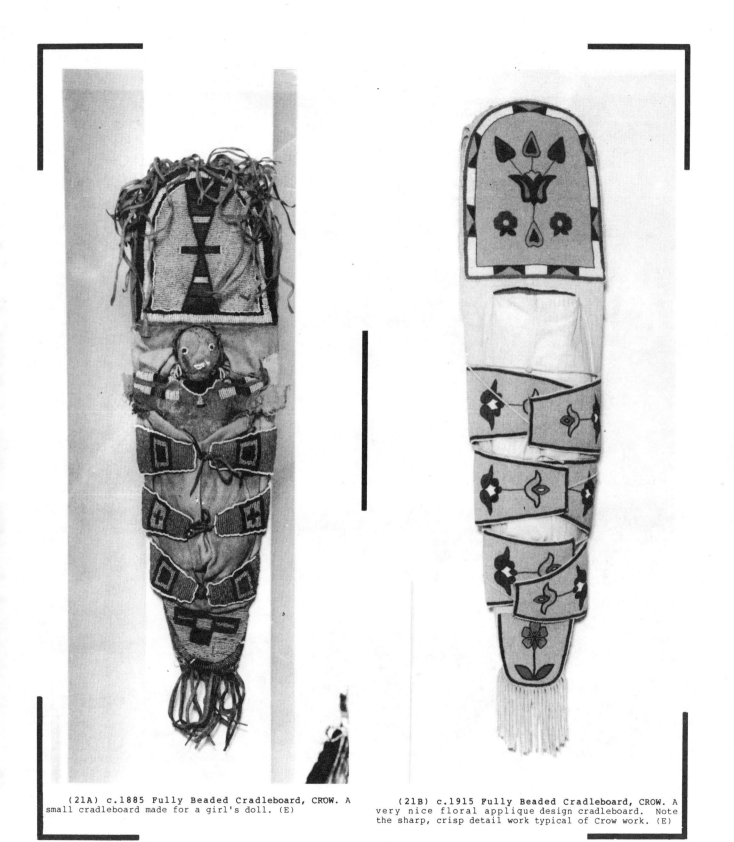

(21A) c.1885 Fully Beaded Cradleboard, CROW. A small cradleboard made for a girl's doll. (E)

(21B) c.1915 Fully Beaded Cradleboard, CROW. A very nice floral applique design cradleboard. Note the sharp, crisp detail work typical of Crow work. (E)

(22A) c.1875 Fully Beaded Cradleboard, SIOUX. N. Fedder calls this a
"classic Sioux cradle." Fully beaded buckskin cover sewn with sinew in lazy
stitch.
　　BELOW: Bottom of cradle. Note use of hawk bells and dentelium shell. (C)

DESIGNS

For the beginning beadworker it is a very good idea to start with simple designs and small projects. Also, copying a design from a piece of Indian beadwork that has appeal to you is better than trying to make up original patterns in the beginning. The creations of credible "Indian" designs can be done by people with considerable experience and study but it takes time and work to achieve this. In some ways it is a good idea to develop these skills along the same way that Native American patterns have evolved.

The ability to create different kinds of designs is, to some extent, dependent upon the environment. There is much more to it of course, but still only materials that are available in your locale or that can be traded can be used. This goes a long way to explain the kinds of designs that were made by Indian people in the past.

Before the importation of glass beads most ornamentation was done with porcupine quills sewn onto leather with sinew. This is no easy task and the resulting designs are truly remarkable. When the first beads small enough for ornamentation purposes were brought in and traded, the People continued to create geometric designs that had worked well with quills. The size of these pony beads had limitations and designs tended to be very simple when compared to what was possible with the smaller seed beads that came later. As can be seen in many of the examples shown in this book, the designs that can be made with seed beads are limited only by the imagination of the beadworker.

Designs often reflect tribal differences. The geometric designs of the Sioux and other Plains Nations, compared to floral designs of the Ojibwa and other Woodland Tribes, provides a good example. However, one must be very careful about attaching tribal labels to beadwork pieces. It was not uncommon for a Shoshone man to possess some Crow beadwork acquired through trade and/or Blackfoot work collected in warfare. Further, as a majority of the Tribes were mobile, trade among many of them was fairly common and with the advent of the European this process was accelerated. For these, and other reasons, scholars who have devoted lifetimes to the problems of "authentication" report that tribal identification is, at best, difficult. This, however, does little to dissuade the vast number of "rendezvous experts" who seem to "know" all there is to know about traditional craftwork.

SIGNIFICANCE

Another subject of conjecture is the significance of different designs. To begin with, spirituality is part of everyday life for the American Indian; it is not something which is simply practiced on Sunday or thought about in a structured manner. Also, one the tenets of the culture is a fierce independence of the individual members. Therefore, when a design is created, whether by vision quest, dream or whatever, it may have a personal spiritual significance. The way it is made manifest (i.e.,the beaded article) will have some relationship to other items beaded by other craftspersons in the Tribe (those are the people who taught the art and the techniques of the craft), but the significance or meaning of the design is personal and as such is beyond communication; neither is any such communication required or expected by other Tribal members. Further, one person may use a symbol, an "arrow" for example, to signify the path to the buffalo hunt, whereas another person can use the same symbol to signify "North," from where the cold comes, and another to mean the death of an enemy. It is also possible, for the culture has plenty of room for it, that a craftsperson creates a design simply because it has an intrinsic beauty in it for the woman making it; she may have been influenced by something or simply thought it up. In other words, it may not mean anything.

If you would like to test this idea, take five old beaded Shoshone articles to five elder Shoshone people and ask them the significance of the designs (PLEASE do not do this unless you know the people very well and are sure· that you are not intruding - there are enough social "scientists" bothering them at present). You will probably get at least five different responses and if you do get a single answer more than once it will be that the meaning is subjective and does not have a Tribal significance.

In general then, **craftwork is not "sign language" that has a societal function;** *it is a personal manifestation.* There is one book, commissioned by the Bureau of Indian Affairs, that uses twenty pages in explaining what each beadwork symbol means to the Sioux Nation. What it really tells the reader is the significance of certain designs to **one** Sioux beadworker for, in truth, they have no "National Meaning." A much more accurate report is given in a foot- note in the Wildschut book mentioned in the *Notes* at the end of this book: After an intensive study by scholar Robert Lowie,

(24A) c.1835 Man's Shirt, SIOUX. Classic example of early design made with trade cloth, pony beads, sinew and paint. Note use of horse hair. (E)

(25A) c.1875 Cradle Board Cover, ASSINIBOINE. U- shaped moose hide cover with cloth applique and floral beading. All sewn with thread. 29 x 62.5 cm. (C)

(25B) c.1905 Beaded Bag, SIOUX. Very nice bag with white background. Stitch may be modified lazy or "crow stitch" from look of lines. (E)

he " . . . found Crow designs and color symbolism to be meager and in most cases quite subjective." In other words they only had meaning to the person who created them.

One final note is needed on the "meaning" of designs. Beadwork designs are, in the Western way of thinking, "personal property." If you borrow one, there is a debt that should be paid. If one is used that was created by an acquaintance, it is proper first to ask for permission to borrow it and then bestow an unsolicited gift on the creator when the project has been completed. If you use a design that came from the Winnebago Nation, but do not know the individual it came from, at the very least you should study and learn about these People in an attempt to understand how that design came about. Now, about using designs.

ADORNMENT

Anyone entering an Indian village in 1800 on a typical work day would have found themselves in a fairly drab place. Girls would begin learning beadwork when seven or eight years old as her desirability as a marriage partner depended to some extent on these skills; further, her status in the community was based on her industry and crafts. Still, the time it took for decorating had to fit into a very busy schedule and therefore quilled and beaded articles were usually either ceremonial or "best dress." When

men hunted, the apparel they wore was not decorated (and it would have been very uncomfortable had it been) and it is certain that the leather dresses worn by the women as they tanned hides were not weighted down with beads. As time and supplies became more plentiful, practical objects were decorated and today it is possible to see everything from beaded salt shakers to fully beaded western boots. Still, the smart craftsman will start small and work up. Something like a head band with a geometric design would be ideal.

In that the process of laying out a design is different in loom work and sewn work it will be explored in those sections but remember to keep away from boredom. First, make sure that a design is used that you like and can live with at least long enough to bead it and hopefully for a long time after that. Second, if the article to be beaded will have a lot of beadwork on it, try to use complimentary designs. On a shirt, for instance, many old photos show that the front and back strips are duplicates, whereas the arm strips are different but complimentary. This will help keep both you and your audience from being bored. Beading is, and should be, a creative experience.

(26A) Contemporary unbacked loom strip. (A)

(27A thru K) c.1983 Hat or Head Bands, SIOUX, CHEYENNE AND CROW. Examples of contemporary geometric loom strips. Note how different kinds of beads give varied impressions. (A)

LOOM WORK

The most simple form of loom was called a "tension loom." With this device the loom strings of fiber or thread were kept taut by attaching one end to a tree or pole and fastening the other end to the beader's wrist. The *bow loom* works on the same principle, but the types of looms that may be purchased commercially have now become plentiful. *Figure Six* shows just a few of them. Any of these, or one that you make yourself, will work fine but there are a couple of things to consider when choosing a loom.

Make sure that it is sturdy and that the sides do not have any give to them. If one of the popular plastic or metal looms is selected to start with, be sure that it is supported on both sides (as pictured), or there will be problems when it is strung and used. Another good idea is to have a loom that is long enough to show the entire pattern. Many of the small looms are made so that you can roll the finished work off of the loom, but if it is necessary to see the pattern to compare design and color it is much easier to have a loom long enough to show the entire piece.

Also, it is advantageous many times to start beading from the middle of the piece (this can be done with almost any design) so that you will have a finished beaded article of the right length. This is difficult on a loom that does not allow you to see all of the beading.

From top to bottom below: (A) 12" metal spring-type loom; (B) 24" wood loom that may be used for 48" loom strips; (C) small 12" wood loom; and, (D) 24" wood spring-type loom with rollers for excess beading.

FIGURE SIX

(29A thru F) c.1983 Hat or Head Bands, SIOUX. Note that A, B, E & F are
the same pattern using different colored beads. B with 12/° and E with
10/°.(A)

It is probably a good idea to buy one of the small looms that are available when you first start beading. They are fairly inexpensive and will give you enough experience to judge just what you want to use as you perfect your skill.

MAKING A LOOM

After you have decided just what you want out of your loom and how big it should be, it is fairly easy to construct one. Keep in mind that you need a sturdy construction and you should always use wood screws and wood glue instead of nails. Be careful about the wood that you choose, making sure that it is perfectly flat and "true."

As stated above, the size of the loom is up to the craftsperson and figures given here are simply examples.

Suppose you want to bead a 28" belt that is two inches wide and need a loom for that purpose. You can use either 1" x 3" or 1" x 4" wood, but the latter is probably better as it will give you more area on the bottom and thus more stability. You do not want the wood to be much wider than your work or the sides will get in your way when you bead the ends. If you want to spend the extra money, hard woods are better as they tend to be straighter wood, and stay that way, but pine will suffice as long as you insure that it is straight and without curves and "bows."

For this loom you will need one piece of wood 36" long for the base and

29

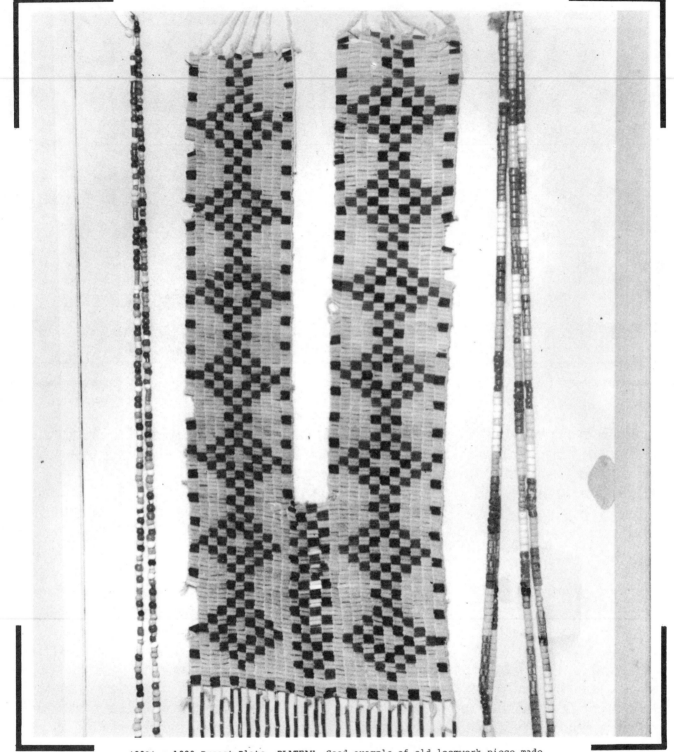

(30A) c.1890 Breast Plate, PLATEAU. Good example of old loomwork piece made with bugle beads. Note Hudson's Bay bead tubes at bottom, Italian Crow Beads on right and Pony or "real" Beads on left. (E)

two pieces three inches long each for the ends. You will also need four wood screws approximately 2" long, some wood glue and two medium sized finishing nails.

As shown in *Figure 7*, use two of the screws and some wood glue to mount each of the end pieces about 3" from the ends of the loom. Make sure that the end piece is screwed down securely and do not use the loom until the glue has set (usually 24 hours). In the exact middle of each end hammer in one of the finishing nails leaving 1" of the nail exposed.

It is very common to see "thread guides" either grooved into the end pieces or mounted to them to use when you string your loom. In *Figure 6*, looms "A" and "D" have springs for guides and loom "C" has grooves made into the end piece. If you choose to use permanent guides you can make small grooves in the wood, mount a spring or use a plastic comb turned upside down with about 1/4" of the teeth showing above the side piece. However, another good method

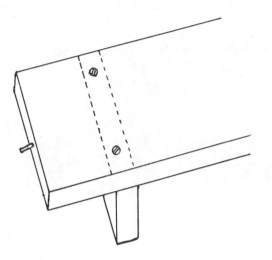

FIGURE 7

(31A thru D) Loomed Beaded Belts, KIOWA. Made by Mr. & Mrs. Alfred Franklin, Jr., all are of 13/° Czech cut beads except "B" that is made of 12/° Japanese cut beads. (F)

(32A) c.1905 Loomed Shirt, NORTHERN PLAINS. Shirt that was loomed in geometric design with 3/4" bugle beads including fringe. (E)

(32B) c.1885 Ball, SIOUX. Fully beaded toy ball made with seed beads. An applique return stitch was used with thread. (E)

(32C) c.1890 Saddle Bag, BLACKFEET. Made on brain-tanned buckskin with trade cloth trim. Beaded with applique running stitch technique. (E)

(33A thru D) c.1982 Loomed Belt Strips, UTE RESERVATION. Made by Millie Etheredge using a variety of beads. From top to bottom: 12/° 3-cut beads, Bugle Beads, 11/° transparent seed beads and 10/° opaque seed beads. (H - Bev & Millie's Curio Shop)

offers some flexibility that you do not get from any of the above and this is illustrated in *Figure 8*.

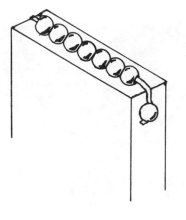

FIGURE 8

To use this method you place a tack about 1/2" below the top of the end piece. Attach a thread to this and just past the point where the thread comes over the top of the end make a large knot - large enough so that your beads will not go through it. Then string the size beads you are going to be using on this thread until you reach the other side and make another knot and then tie the thread around another tack. The loom threads will be guided between these beads, so they should not be crowded together on the string.

The biggest advantage to this method is that you use the same size beads at the end as what you are going to use; if you are going to be beading with bugle beads, you use bugles at the ends and with size 12/° seed beads, you use them at the ends, etc. In this way you do not have the problem of having your loom threads being pulled in or out by your beadwork. Also, if you use a loom like *Figure 6B* that is made so that you can pull your work around the loom as you finish with it (meaning that you can do 48" of beadwork on a 24" loom), this guide can be removed easily when you want to move your work.

STRINGING

Before threading the loom it is necessary to identify the threads. The long thread that is strung onto the loom is often called the "*warp*" thread and the thread that is beaded with is called the "*weft*" thread. These are names that come from weaving and after a few pages of warping and wefting it is easy to become confused. The long thread that is strung on the loom will be called simply the **loom thread** and the thread that you use for beading will be called the **beading thread**.

In order to string the loom threads, tie the end of the thread to the nail at the end of the loom and start in the middle. As noted in the *General Information*, nymo thread is good for this and size "D" will give enough strength. Hold the spool of thread in your hand and let the thread come between your fingers; do not take the thread off of the side of the spool as that puts twists into it and weakens the thread over time. You can wait until all of the loom threads are in place to use the bees wax, but if the

thread is waxed while stringing the loom it is easier to give a more uniform application.

After the first loom thread is strung, do not cut it. Wrap it around the nail at the other end and then string the thread left of center. When that thread is in place go around the nail at the end and string the thread right of center and so forth moving one string out from the middle with each thread until you reach the outside, or final strings. If extra strength is needed, as with a belt, it is a good idea to have a double loom thread on both of the outside strings of the project. **Remember that the beads go in between the loom threads**, so if the design is 13 beads wide, there will be 14 loom threads, etc. **It is always a good idea to use an odd number of beads** as this provides a center to your work. As the loom is strung, careful attention must be made to how taut the loom strings are; there should be the same amount of

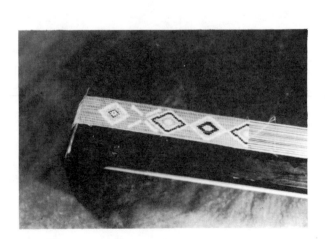

FIGURE 9

34

tension on each loom thread. The idea is to have them tight, so that there is no slack in them, but remember that they are not guitar strings. If, after stringing the loom, you find that one of the strings is too loose, tighten that string by tying a piece of thread around the slack loom thread just above the nail and pulling down gently until it has the proper tension. Then wrap the thread around the nail and knot securely.

BEADING

Before beading begins, there is a need to consider the design. The best tool to use is graph paper as it will allow you to map out the design in detail.

Find a design you like and copy it onto your graph paper. A set of colored pencils works well for this, or symbols may be used for the different colors that are going to be used. If the design will be repeated in the piece, you need only copy it once.

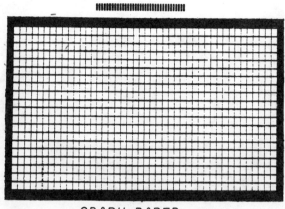

GRAPH PAPER

The use of bead graph paper, when designs are created or modified (made

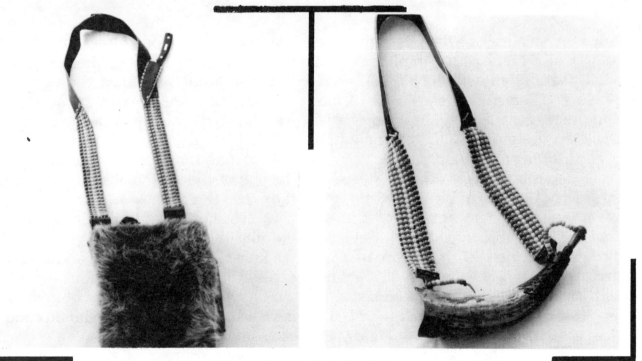

(35A & B) c.1982 Loom Straps. Attractive loomed straps made by Ray Ginther with Crow Beads, Leather Thongs and Imitation Sinew. (H)

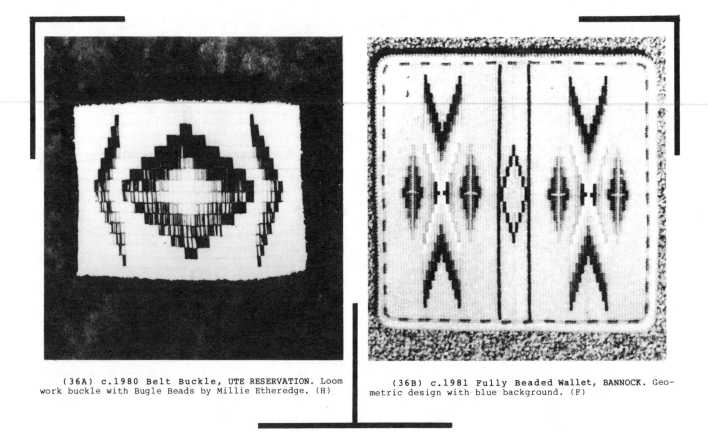

(36A) c.1980 Belt Buckle, UTE RESERVATION. Loom work buckle with Bugle Beads by Millie Etheredge. (H)

(36B) c.1981 Fully Beaded Wallet, BANNOCK. Geometric design with blue background. (F)

larger or smaller or when changing the colors), also gives you a graphic view at what the design will look like before beading. Remember, start with something that is challenging, but managable. Once the design is plotted on the graph paper, beading may begin.

Begin by cutting off a 24" piece of thread. Make the cut clean so that there are no ragged edges and make it at an angle. Wax the thread and put this through your needle. If you are using a size 10/^{0} bead, "D" nymo will be fine, with smaller beads it would be better to use "B" or "A" thread. Match the needle size to the bead and thread size, as described in the *General Information* Section. For general loom work, use a long or "beading" needle. All of the

beading will be done by leaving a single thread running through the beads each time the needle is pulled through. The needle, therefore, should be at a point less than halfway down the length of the whole thread. Now tie the long end of the beading thread just made to eight of the outmost loom threads; **do not cut off the excess thread**.

To start beading the design, follow the illustration shown in *Figure 11*. Tie the knot to the loom thread, and press the excess thread along the loom thread in the direction of the beading; both threads have been waxed and they should cling to each other.

Nymo thread is great for beading because of its strength. However, nylon knots tend to slip, but if you bead over the

(37A thru J) c.1982 Loom Strips, SIOUX and CHEYENNE. Assorted designs and styles of loomwork strips. All are unbacked for hat or head bands. (A)

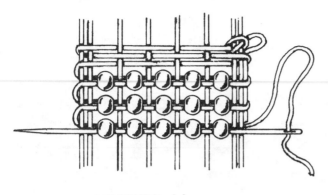

FIGURE 11

come back by going over the threads you came under and under the threads you went over. In that there are an uneven number of threads this will work out just right. Do this three or four times to insure that the beadwork does not unravel when it is taken off the loom. Make sure that you end up so that your beading thread has to go under the loom threads for the next weave.

Next, take the beading thread down and over the outside loom thread. String the proper amount of beads on the beading thread, and from the bottom, press the beads up between the proper loom thread. While holding the beads in place by pressing up with a finger under all of the beads, pull the beading thread taut, take it up over the outside loom

excess thread in every knot made it will insure that the threads stay tied.

Now weave the thread over the next loom thread in, and then under the next one and so forth until you get to the outside thread. Go over that one, and

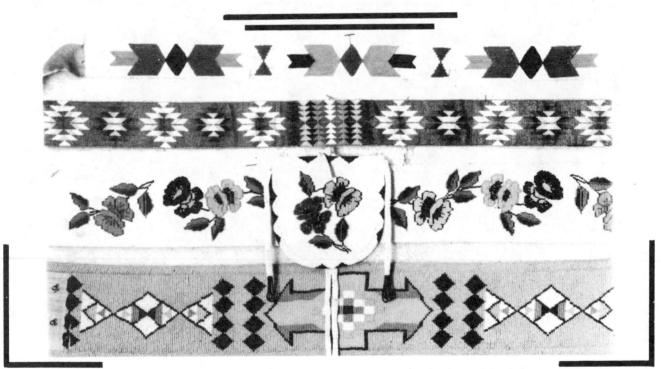

(38A thru D) c.1983 Loomed Belts, SHOSHONE and ARAPAHO. Variety of beaded designs in assorted width; all are backed. Note bead wrapping on purse dangles. Belt "B" is Arapaho made by Helene B. Furlong. (F)

(39A thru D) c.1982 Loomed Belts, UTE RESERVATION. Made by Millie Etheredge, "C" is made with 15/° Hexigons and "D" with 12/° 3-cut beads. (H- Bev & Millie's Curio Shop, Roosevelt, Utah.

thread and go back through the bead on top of the loom thread. There are now two beading threads through each bead; one under the loom threads and one over each one. The next row of beads is done in exactly the same way. The only reason to start from the bottom on each row is that it is easier. It is a good idea to keep the graph paper handy so that the design can be referred to often.

Note that nothing is said about going either left to right, or right to left. First, as long as you go under the loom threads with the first pass and through the beads over these threads on the second it does not matter if you are going left or right. Second, if you are left handed you will tend to work left to right and if right handed the other way around. Either will do nicely. And, third, if you get tired of going one way, turn the loom around and go the other.

As explained above, when the beads are placed on the loom the beading thread is pulled "taut." The beads should be snug against each other, but not tight. When the beading is finished and before it is sewn to cloth or leather, the beads should roll like ball bearings. Further, if you are forced to use a color of beads that is slightly smaller than the others, the rows that these beads are in will have to be less taut than rows that do not have them included. **The width of loomwork is**

always gauged by the size of the largest beads.

As inexact as the above sounds, it will become easier to gain uniformity with experience. It is easy at this point, however, to see why the selection of uniform beads is so important in the work. As you select the beads that are uniform, place the ones that are too large or too small back in the craft box for later use. The beads that come in weird shapes or that have a hole too small to accept the needle should be thrown away.

When there is enough beading thread left on the needle to bead about three more rows, cut another beading thread, wax and knot to the outside loom thread. Lay the excess thread from the knot along side the loom thread, and continue beading over this excess thread. Bead the next two rows, and then cut the beading thread so that it will go about three-quarters of the way through the beads. Take the needle back through the row that was just completed so that the thread comes off and is hidden inside these beads. Now put the needle on the new beading thread that was tied to the loom thread two rows back. Run this through the two beaded rows making

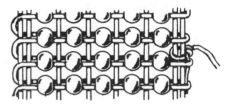

FIGURE 12

(40A) c.1955 Loomed Belt with Buckle, UTE. Nice loomed dancing belt and matching buckle made with 11/° seed beads. Note edging style on both. (B)

sure that when you exit the last row it goes over and down under the loom thread for the next row of beads. Continue this way until the end of the project is reached.

A few words about the length of the beading thread: It may be that 24" is either too long or too short and a bit of experimentation will give the length that is best for your kind of work. If a longer thread is used it requires less knotting, but tends to tangle. If this is the case, simply wax the thread again until it will remain straight.

At the end of the beaded strip, repeat what was done at the beginning. Weave the thread through the loom thread a number of times and knot securely as shown in *Figure 13*.

If you ever have to replace a bead

Figure 13

in the middle of your work, do it exactly as you did when you started a new beading thread. Start two rows before the bead and continue for two rows after it has been put in place.

VARIATIONS

There are a number of techniques that can be used in loomwork and the following may be worth considering.

(41A thru D) c.1950 Loomed Articles, UTE. Barretts, Purse and Headband are all loomed with 10/° seed beads. Note different styles of edging used on barretts. (B)

As mentioned above, many times it is necessary to bead an article that must be of an exact length such as a belt or head band. This is usually easier to do if the beading is started in the middle. Although the methods explained above will most often be used, the technique for starting the strip is different.

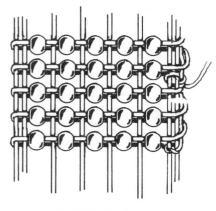

FIGURE 14

As shown in *Figure 14*, in the exact middle of the loom, tie a beading thread to the outside loom thread and press the excess thread from the knot against the loom thread. Then, about the width of two beads away, tie another beading thread to the loom thread and, after pressing the excess knot thread to the loom thread, let this thread hang down and begin beading. When the first half is completed, weave the beading thread through the loom threads as explained above and return to the middle section. Place the needle on the beading thread that was left hanging near the center and go back through the two rows that have been completed making sure that the needle emerges from the center row so that it will go down over the outside loom thread and start working on that

(42A) c.1978 Doll. Made by Tom Domiani, note loomed strips on shoulders. (H - Boyer's Indian Arts & Crafts, Jackson, WY.)

(42B) c.1975 Buckskin Dress, WINNEBAGO. Worn by Neola Walker, note loomed bead strips on dress and matching headband. (A)

side of the strip. This is finished off exactly like the other side.

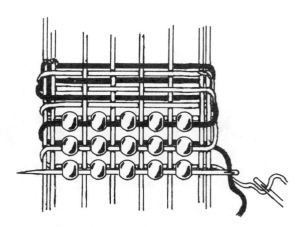

FIGURE 15

Another variation that works well is loomwork with two needles. *Figure 15* shows that you start as with regular beading, but instead of tying one beading thread to the outside loom thread at the start, you tie one thread at each side. These are woven as before but toward each other. When approximately three "weaves" have been made the beading may begin. String the proper amount of beads on one of the threads, take it under the loom threads, push the beads into place and then use the other beading thread to go through the beads, making sure that this goes over all of the loom threads. String the needed number and colors of beads on this same thread, take it under the loom thread and, from the bottom, push the beads into place. Now the other beading thread is taken through the beads and so forth. There are a number of advantages to this technique in that the loom work goes

(43A) c.1978 Bandolier, KIOWA. This brown bandolier is made of 12/° Japanese Cut Beads. (F)

(44A thru C) c.1975 Belt Buckels, SIOUX, YAKIMA & ARAPAHO. Examples of Applique technique when used on contemporary belt buckles. (A)

(44D thru H) c.1982 Loomed Belt Strips, UTE RESERVATION. Made by Millie Etheredge, these are excellent examples of loom work. All belts are without backing. (H)

44

faster, and as you are able to pull the beads "taut" when they are on the loom with a thread at each end, it is easier to keep the rows even and straight.

Another variation, of course, is to use both the two needle technique and start in the middle of the project. Whatever method works best and is used, the following steps may also be used.

ENDINGS

In place of the uniform, straight ends of regular loomwork, there are a number of variations that are possible. Most of these methods use exactly the same looming stitch used above and it takes little imagination to come up with others that will look good.

Figure 16A shows an extended "V." *Figure 16B* is a technique that may be used to make a beaded strip either wider or narrower. To make a fancy head band, the loom is strung with 14 loom threads but at each end only the middle 10 are used, nine beads wide. Then in the middle (the brow band) all 14 strings are used, 13 beads wide, etc. If any of the methods in this section are used, when the piece is removed from the loom the excess loom thread is placed on a needle and woven back through the beads. When the project is sewn in place, make sure the end beads are sewn securely.

Figure 16C shows an inverted "V" and *16D* shows how to make any number of "dangles" at the end of your beaded piece.

Shown in *Figure 16E* is a variation

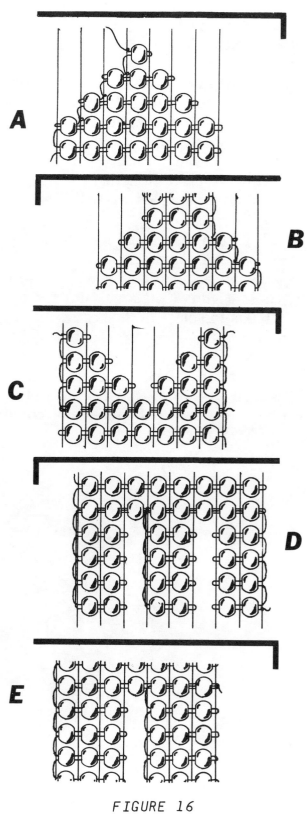

A

B

C

D

E

FIGURE 16

that is useful in making a necklace. In this method, if the piece is 15 beads wide, you simply leave out the middle bead and continue up both sides with strips that are seven beads wide. When the end is reached, it is a simple matter to sew the two 7-bead row strips together giving a look of a continual beaded strip. The ends can be sewn together using the extended loom threads or with another beading thread.

With the beaded strip complete and the ends woven as described, the project can now be taken off of the loom. As shown in *Figure 13* (above), do not cut the threads too close to the beadwork but leave two or three inches of loom threads extending. If the work is not going to be mounted immediately, it is a good idea to place tape over the exposed threads to insure that the work does not come apart. (See *Figure 17*)

BACKING

It is possible to use the beadwork without backing, but sewing the strip on to cloth or leather is relatively easy.

Before nymo became popular it was always advisable to have a piece of leather or cloth between the beading and the leather to which it was sewn. This gives the thread a better chance of lasting longer as it lessens the stress caused by the leather stretching. Nymo, however, has some stretch to it and thus it is only necessary to back your piece with leather if you prefer to do so. However, many craftspersons like to mount their beadwork on leather before sewing it to the article, as most items wear out before the beading. It is much easier to place the beadwork on another article this way.

The use of a sewing machine is not

FIGURE 17 – c.1979 Unbacked Loom Stip. Example of using tape to keep threads from coming apart on finished piece. (A)

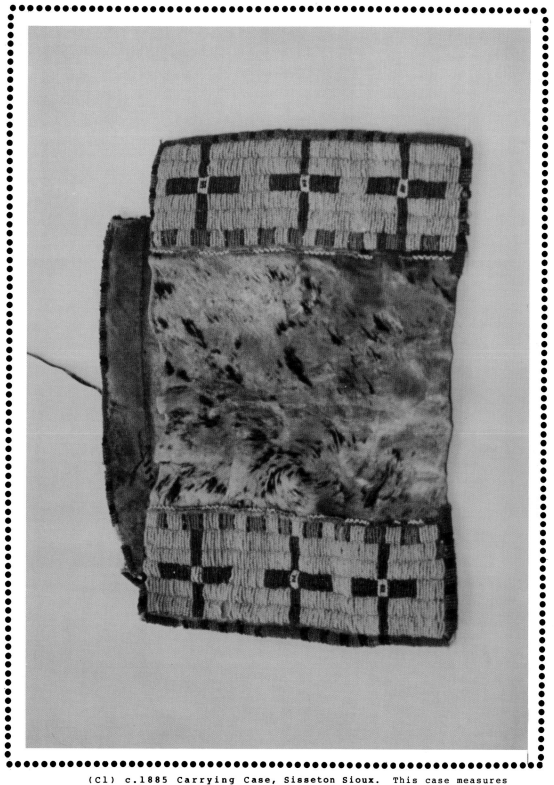

(C1) c.1885 **Carrying Case, Sisseton Sioux.** This case measures approximately 14 x 10 inches. It is sewn with sinew, made of very thick buffalo hide and features "greasy" yellow beads. The adornment of four (4) tin cones and horsehair have become detached with use. (A)

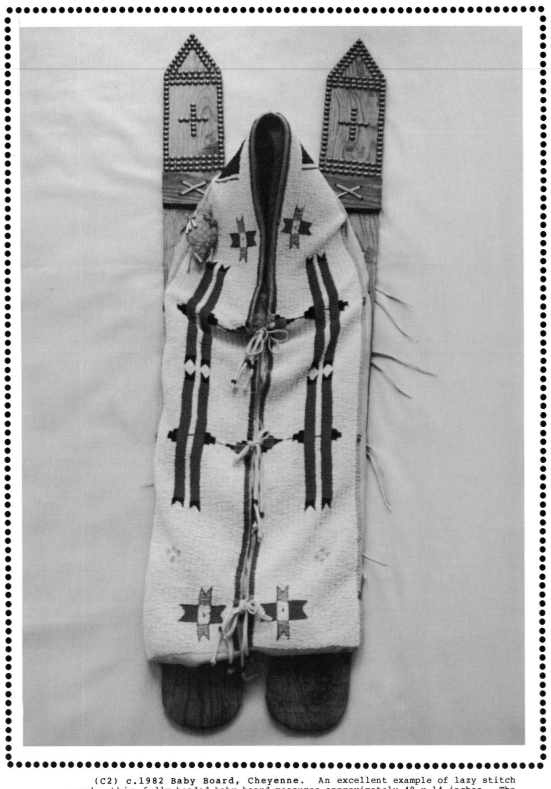

(C2) c.1982 Baby Board, Cheyenne. An excellent example of lazy stitch work, this fully beaded baby board measures approximately 48 x 14 inches. The fetish is done in an applique stitch. The board was constructed by Gerald Van Sickle and the beading done by his wife, Michele. (G)

(C3) c.1960 Loom Work Purse, Ute Reservation. An outstanding example of some of the possibilities of loom work. The purse is approximately 12 x 10 inches. Made by Millie Etheredge, this is the product of three years of working "when there was time." Made of 10/° seed beads. (H)

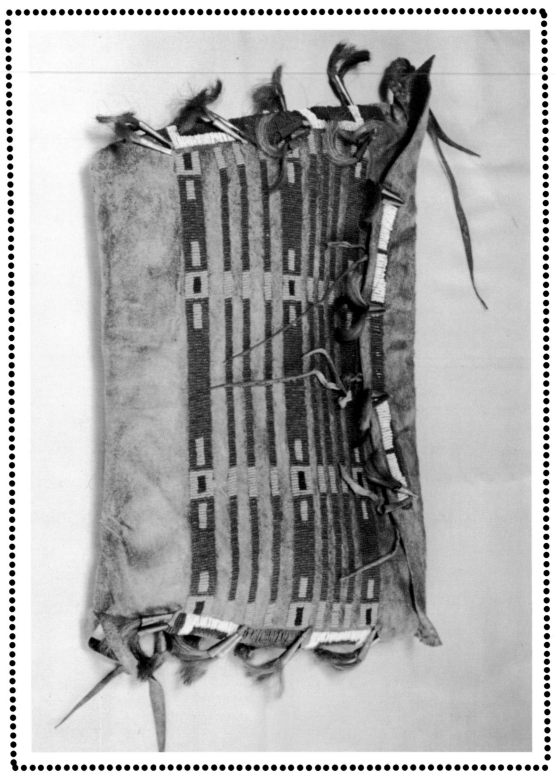

(C4) c.1875 Saddle Storage Bag, Sioux. Beaded on brain-tanned buckskin, the bag is sewn with sinew across the bottom and up the sides. The flap is closed with thong ties and is adorned with tin cones and horsehair fringes. The bag measures 32 x 55 cm. (C)

really advisable unless it is possible to find a machine that can be adjusted to match the length of the rows. It is much better to sew the beadwork on by hand. It is helpful, however, to use a sewing machine without thread in it to make holes that can be used when sewing the beadwork to the leather. Just make sure that as the beadwork is sewn on that everything is securely sewn. Over time, the item that has been beaded and the nylon thread in the beading may stretch, and you will want to go back over the piece and sew any places that show stress or stretch. Be sure when the beadwork is sewn on to the object being made that the loom threads are all securely hidden under the beadwork.

One word of caution - **Do Not** use glue or cement to hold the beadwork to leather or any other material! In the short run it might appear easier, but glue is a modern invention that is best done

without. It may be that a very small spot of glue may be helpful in holding two pieces together while they are sewn securely in place, but that is the most that should ever be used. The vision of dried glue showing through a nice piece of loomwork or the strip of dried glue that is left on leather to remind the wearer of "short run ease" simply does not justify using this shortcut. Like the thornbird, the sweetest song requires some sacrifice.

The uses of loomwork are many, and the pictures that follow this section illustrate just some of them. The Ute purse in the color photos is a great example of how loomwork can be used. You might want to compare some of the loomed belt buckles shown in this section with those that have been appliqued in other sections of this book.

(47A thru C) c.1977 Loomed Buckles and Barrett. Note edge style on barrett made by Virginia Free (Winnebago). (A)

(47D) c.1981 Loomed Barrett. Made by Ann Szabo, this sunburst design shows some of the flexibility of loom work. Note use of peyote stitch and "dangles" on barrett stick. (A)

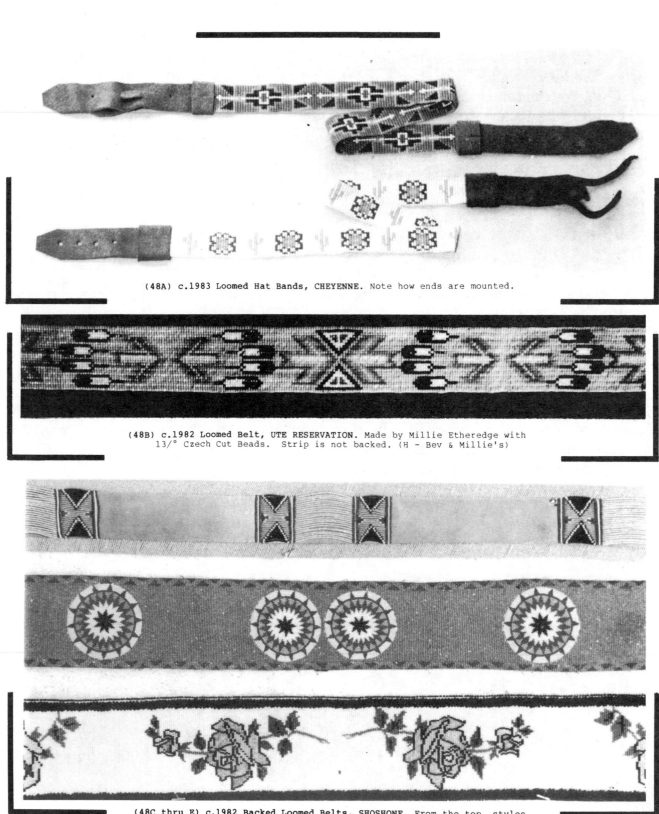

(48A) c.1983 Loomed Hat Bands, CHEYENNE. Note how ends are mounted.

(48B) c.1982 Loomed Belt, UTE RESERVATION. Made by Millie Etheredge with 13/° Czech Cut Beads. Strip is not backed. (H - Bev & Millie's)

(48C thru E) c.1982 Backed Loomed Belts, SHOSHONE. From the top, styles shown are hand-beading, applique stitch (note that rosettes are made using the technique descibed in the rosette section) and floral loomwork. (F)

(49A) c.1983 **Belt and Knife Sheath.** Excellent craftsmanship showing three styles of beading: (1) Belt is loomed, (2) Sheath body is done with Lazy Stitch and (3) Top of Sheath is done with applique. (G)

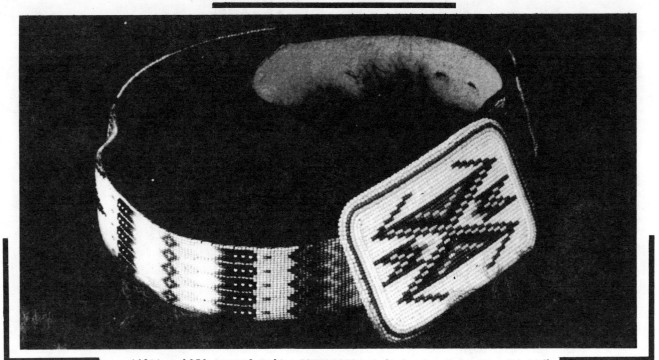

(49B) c.1979 **Loomed Belt, COMMANCHE.** Made by Jr. Weryackwe with 13/° Czeck cut beads. (49C) c.1981 **Belt Buckle, CHIPPEWA-CREE.** A gift to the author from the Standing Rock family made of 12/° Japanese cut beads. (A)

(50A thru C) **Blanket Stips.** Dates and Ethnology unknown. The top strip
is done with porcupine quills. (E)

APPLIQUE

SINEW

Before the introduction of needles and thread all quill and beadwork was done with sinew. From a buffalo, elk or any large animal, the sinew was taken from the large tendon which lies along each side of the back bone, beginning just back of the neck and extending toward the rear. Depending upon the size of the animal this sinew may be up to a yard long and, of course, the longer the sinew the better. While the majority of beadwork is now done using the more modern tools available, some craftspersons still use sinew. It can be purchased from many of the major Indian craft suppliers or produced by following these steps.

After the tendon has been removed from the animal, but while it is still moist, it should be cleaned thoroughly by first scraping it with a piece of bone or the back of a skinning knife. Then it is placed in water and left to soak until it appears white and is completely flexible. It is important that as much of the natural glue as possible has been removed from it. When the tendon is completely flexible insert an awl or nail between the thread-

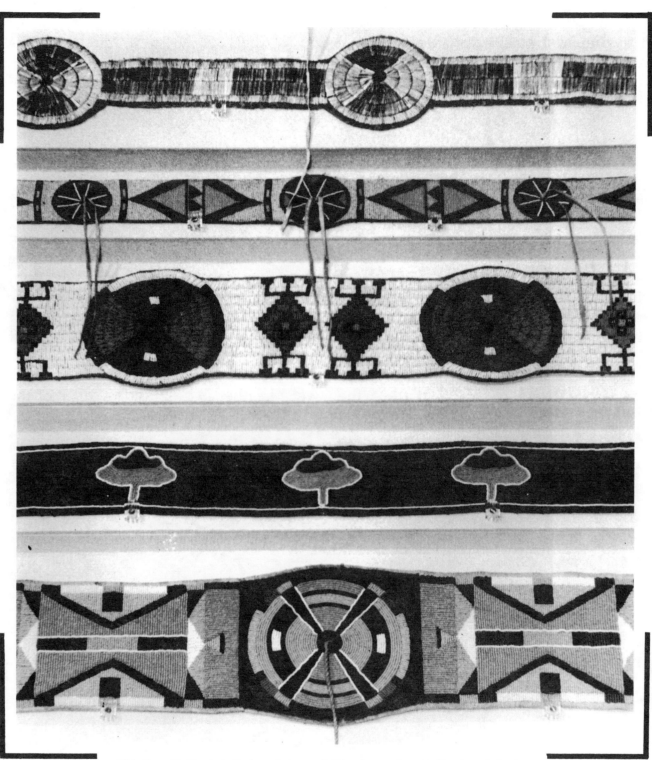

(51A thru E) **Blanket Strips.** Dates and Ethnology unknown. The top strip is
done with porcupine quills. (E)

like sinew and strip them off one by one. The prepared sinew can then be made into a braid loose enough to allow drawing them out as needed. Then wrap the braid carefully until it is to be used.

In order to sew with sinew, it is necessary to make a small hole in the leather with an awl or sharp object. To prepare the sinew fibers, just prior to use an end is moistened with saliva, twisted to a small point and allowed to dry hard. Several of these threads should be prepared before starting. As the sinew is used it is held in the mouth to make it flexible again; if it is more palatable to use a shallow cup of water, make sure that the pointed end is not allowed to get wet. Sinew is an excellent thread for beading and in many old museum pieces the sinew looks like it is part of the leather.

Any of the techniques in this chapter may be done using either sinew or thread but, as the vast majority of beadwork is done with thread, the use of that product will be used for illustrations.

MATERIALS

The material the beadwork is sewn to does not change the stitches that are used. However, it may change how tight you sew the beads; in no case should the material ever bunch up because of your stitch. If cloth is used make sure that it does not stretch. Felt or canvas work well, but if wool is used do not let it get wet. Leather is best, and because of the

(52A) c.1905 Shirt, SIOUX. Fully beaded lazy stitch shirt. Note cotton bottom strips and leather sleeve ties. (E)

(53A) c.1890 Buckskin Shirts,(Left) UTE. Smoked brain-tanned buckskin shirt with narrow strips of lozy stitch beadwork. (Right) GROS VENTRE buckskin shirt with wide lazy stitch strips. Note the striking geometric design. (E)

thickness, buckskin is better than elk or cowhide. The ultimate material is brain-tanned buckskin (which is very expensive), as the needle goes through it very easily. Whatever material is used, make sure that you always have a sharp needle. As explained in the *Introduction*, it will be best to use a short, or **Sharps** beading needle, and it is a good idea to change needles as they become dull.

It is also a good idea to have a large flat area with plenty of light on which to work. The material that is being beaded should be kept fairly flat to avoid bunching up and this can be accomplished by tacking it to a frame, backing it with canvas or another piece of leather, or by being careful as it is beaded.

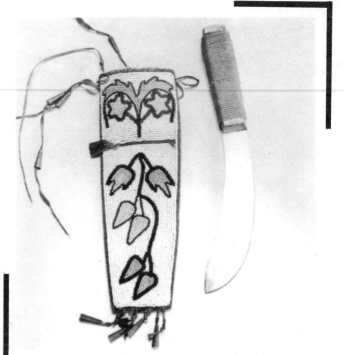

(54A) c.1875 Knife Scabbard and Knife, OJIBWA. Scabbard is cloth lined with white background. Note decorative use of tin cones and wood beads on tassels. Knife is J. Russel and Co., Green River Works. (C)

STITCHES

When sinew is used as the principal thread for beading, it is common for bead workers to sew the beads to the leather

Contemporary   Traditional
FIGURE 18

without going completely through it. Sinew is a fiber made up of smaller fibers and, while extremely tough, it will wear away with constant rubbing. With the introduction of nylon thread, however, the majority of Indian beadwork that is seen today is done by going through the

(54B) c.1880 Knife Scabbard, SIOUX. Beaded buffalo hide, sewn with sinew, with tassels. (54C) c.1900, SIOUX. Beaded rawhide sewn with sinew. Note bead wrapping on tassel. (C)

54

(55A) c.1860 War Shirt, SIOUX. Beaded Shirt with painted yoke. Horse hair fringe is wrapped with quills. Lazy stitch technique is used on both the side strips and "V" shaped neck piece. (E)

FIGURE 19 - Beading is
backed with canvas in these Cree
moccasins

leather. The attractive thing about the
traditional method is that the back of the
beaded piece shows no threads at all and
this may still be done using nymo thread.
In order to prevent rubbing, knots of
sinew are also tied on to the beaded side
of the leather used; today most knots are
hidden on the reverse side.

TECHNIQUES

There are basically two techniques
used in sewn beadwork: The *Overlaid
Stitch* and the *Lazy Stitch*; there are also
variations of these stitches that will be
explained herein. All of these techniques

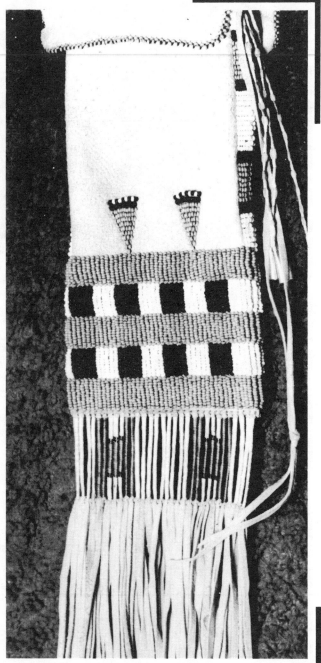

(56A) c.1980 Pipe Bag. Contemporary Cheyenne
style pipe bag beaded on commercial tan buckskin. Made
by Michele VanSickle, the fringe has been quilled.(G)

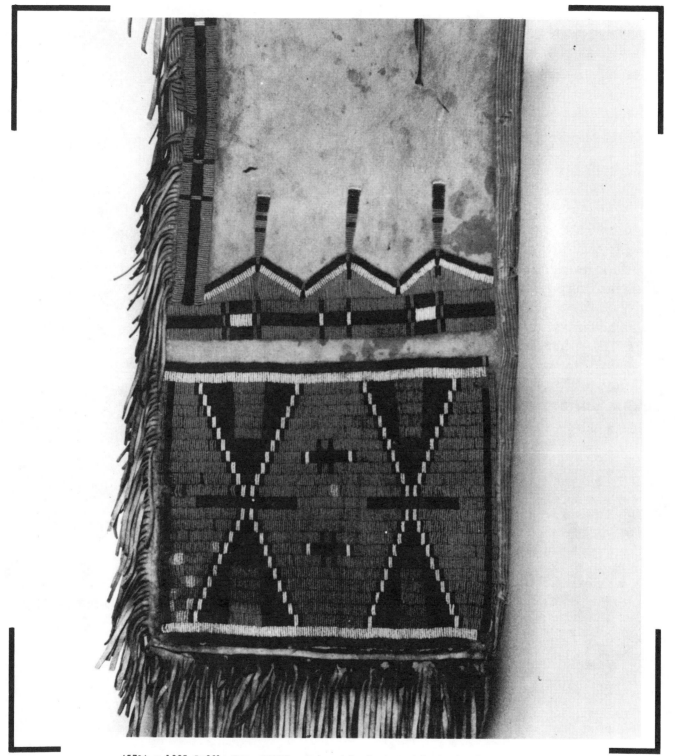

(57A) c.1885 Saddle Bag, SIOUX. Fringed brain-tanned buckskin saddle bag
with geometric, lazy stitch design. Note edging up side of bag. (E)

are called *applique* or *sewn* beadwork as the beads are applied directly to the object being beaded. In the past the overlaid stitch was used by almost every Nation on the North American continent, whereas the lazy stitch was only found west of the Mississippi and seldom seen farther north than just over the Canadian border. Today, however, due to the influence of the Sioux Nation on most facets of Indian life, the lazy stitch is very common in all parts of the country. It is not uncommon to see beaded items that incorporate both of these techniques.

It may be that this stitch is referred to as a "lazy stitch" because it is less firm than the other sewn stitches, because it may pull out more readily than other stitches with wear, or because it is easier and faster to cover large areas than with

LAZY STITCH

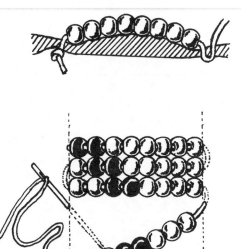

FIGURE 20

(58A) c.1885 Storage Bag, SIOUX. Lazy stitch beaded storage bag with tin cones and horsehair decoration. Note the beaded sides and top flap. (E)

(59A) c.1890 Tobacco Bag, CHEYENNE. Geometric design bag with white seed bead background. (E)

(59B) c.1880 Tobacco Bag, CHEYENNE. Attractive lazy stitch bag with edging on the flap. (E)

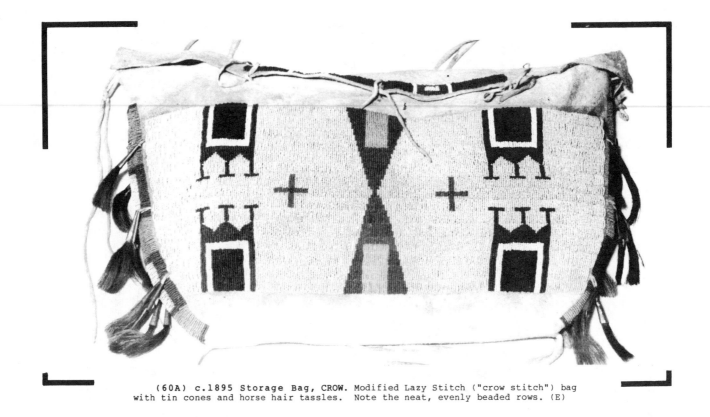

(60A) c.1895 Storage Bag, CROW. Modified Lazy Stitch ("crow stitch") bag with tin cones and horse hair tassles. Note the neat, evenly beaded rows. (E)

the applique stitch shown later. In any event, it is **not**, nor ever was, called the "lazy squaw stitch" by Native Americans. This term is repugnant to many Indians and the proper term is Lazy Stitch.

Again, bead graph paper is ideal for laying out the design before beading begins. Due to the way the beads are laid out, this technique works well with geometric designs but requires a great deal of skill to use for others. Also, if an article will suffer a great deal of use or abuse, it may be well to use one of the other applique stitches in this book.

With the lazy stitch technique, one needle is used and beads are sewn with a single thread. It is a good idea to use the strongest thread possible and if the beads are large enough a "D" Nymo is good for this. Most lazy stitch is done with size $10/^0$ or $11/^0$ beads, but it is also seen with beads as small as $12/^0$ and sometimes with $13/^0$. Also, lazy stitch work was done with pony beads in the 19th century.

As shown in *Figure 20*, beads are applied in a series of bands or rows and the number of beads in each can vary between 5 and 9 according to taste, requirements and bead size. (As shown in the photos, Crow beadwork often uses a great many beads per stitch.) An uneven number will help with many designs and in centering the work. The secret here is not to use too many beads in a single row as the result will not be appealing; rows that are about 3/8" work well.

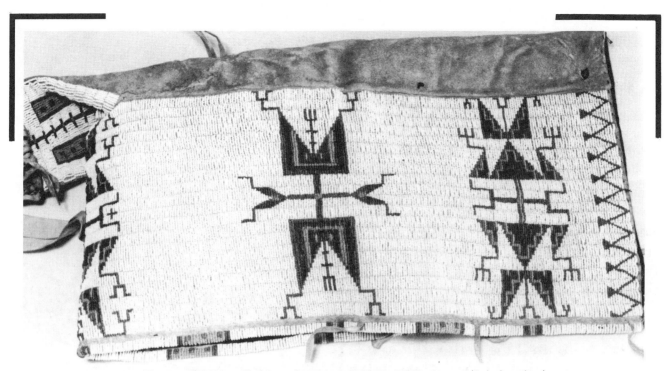

(61A) c.1900 Cradle Board Cover, ROSEBUD SIOUX. Lazy stitched on brain-tanned leather. Colors are blue, red, yellow and green on white background; binding is also covered. Lined with black calico. (C)

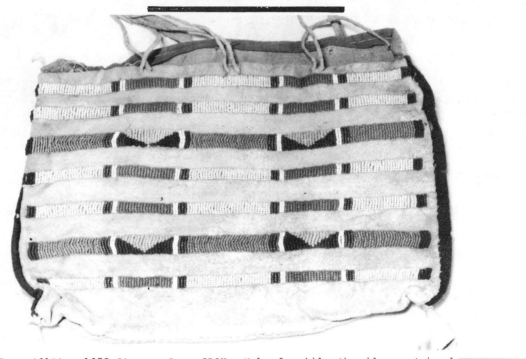

(61B) c.1875 Storage Bag, CROW. Made of cowhide, the sides are trimmed with red trade cloth. Back is made of canvas and colors are light blue, red, white, and medium blue. (C)

After the first beads have been sewn in place the needle is brought back up through the leather next to the last beads sewn on, and the same number are placed on the thread and sewn into place next to them. With the traditional stitch, the needle goes under the surface of the leather, but with a contemporary stitch or if material or canvas is used, the needle passes completely through. If thread is used, waxing is necessary not only to keep the thread straight but because it will help hold the stitch tight while the second stitch is being made. The next stitch is made in the same way, and so forth, until the end of the row is reached. Be sure and keep an eye on the graph paper so that the proper beads are used to form the design.

The next row is made by bringing the thread up almost through the top hole of the row below, and the same number of beads are used as this row is stitched into place. The idea is to create small "ridges" with each row; this is done by crowding the beads on the thread and pulling the stitch tight enough to raise the center bead, but not so tight that the material puckers. In order to get a uniform-looking beaded piece it takes practice and patience, and most bead-workers find that they tear out their first couple of rows after they get the hang of the technique. One of the advantages of sewn beadwork is the ability to replace sections of beading that is not "just right" when the piece is completed. Repair work, as might be imagined, is easier

(62A) c.1890 Bag or Purse, CROW. Crow stitch, sinew sewn bag. Note four different, but complimentary patterns. (E)

(62B) c.1900 Beaded Dress, SIOUX and (62C) c.1890 Beaded Dress, SIOUX. Both dresses have fully beaded yoke and sleeves and use lazy stitch technique. (E)

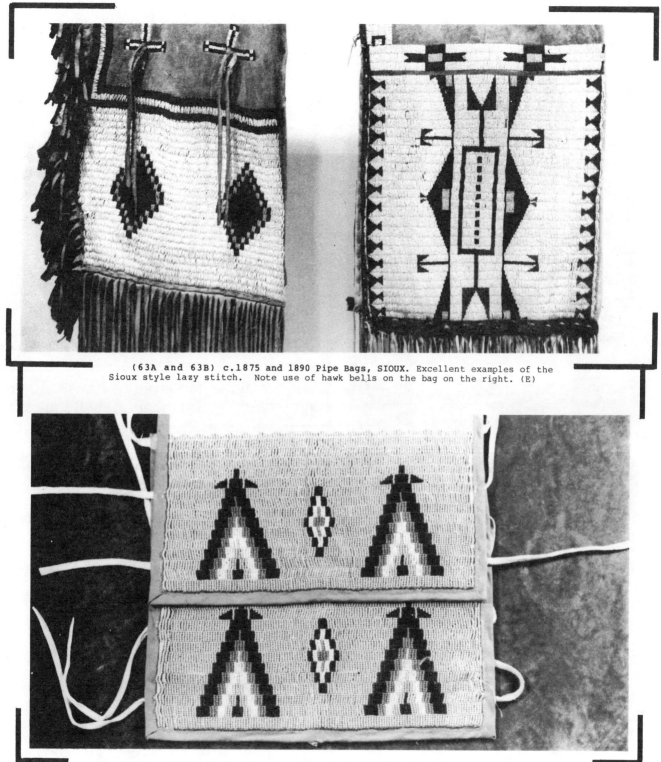

(63A and 63B) c.1875 and 1890 **Pipe Bags, SIOUX.** Excellent examples of the Sioux style lazy stitch. Note use of hawk bells on the bag on the right. (E)

(63C) c.1953 **Beaded Cuffs, UTE.** Lazy stitch cuffs with cloth edges and buckskin thongs. (B)

than with loom work also.

Starting a new beading thread is much easier with applique, but be sure when you knot the old thread, it is neither too tight nor too loose as this will disrupt the flow of your work.

One idea that many beadworkers find useful is to draw one line where the bottom of the lazy stitch is to be started and another at one of the sides. This will help insure that the stitch is always straight and it may even be useful to draw more lines parallel to these if needed. These lines can be drawn on the back of the piece being beaded with a soft lead pencil; with a little wear the lines will disappear. Another help in producing good work is to select the beads carefully before they are strung; beads that are either too large or too small, or those with weird shapes, will quickly destroy the overall effect of the work.

One variation of the lazy stitch is called a **modified lazy stitch** or **crow stitch** as shown in *Figure 21* (below):

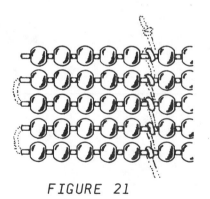

FIGURE 21

With this method enough beads are strung to complete three or four rows on the thread before going back into the material.

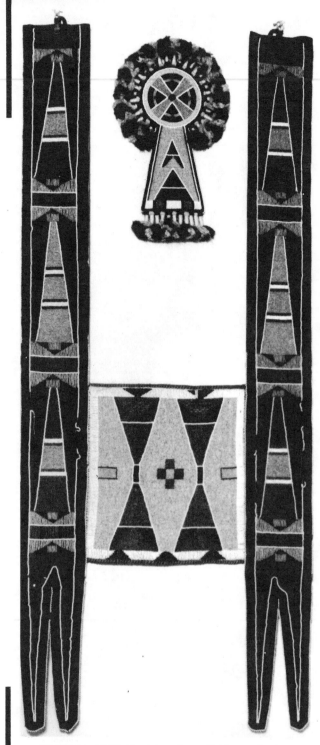

(64A) c.1978 Martingale, CROW. Made by Gary Johnson, this is an excellent example of "Crow Stitch" and applique beadwork. Head piece is woven with horse hair and then beaded. (D)

(65A) c.1980 Lance Scabbard, CROW. Made on rawhide with trade cloth edging and backing. Lance stem is painted. Note the beaded edge on the trade cloth and that the buckskin fringe is wrapped with horse hair. (D)

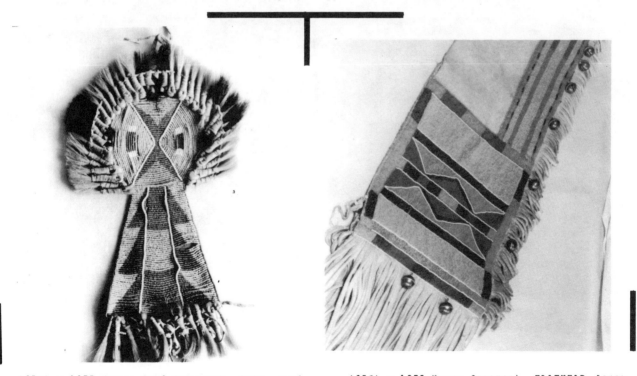

(65B) c.1875 Horse Head Ornament, CROW. Seed beads sewn with sinew onto rawhide. Dyed horsehair fringe around top and at bottom. (C)

(65C) c.1875 Horse Ornament, FLATHEAD. Large, decorated buckskin strip with beading on cloth and buckskin with attached bells. (C)

This is repeated until the project is covered from side to side. The thread is then brought up between the beads that will separate the first row from the second, taken over the thread and back into the material used. This is repeated on the next bead over and then, with the same number of beads, up between rows two and three.

In either of these methods, keep the graphed design handy and at constant reference. Replacement of beads is fairly easy (simply crush the offending bead with the method shown before, take the needle through the leather and beads prior to the missing bead, string a new bead, continue through the remaining beads on that row and go back through the material), but this is bothersome when beading.

OVERLAID

Applique or Overlaid stitches may be used for geometric designs, and is the best possible method to bead the curving lines of the Woodland floral designs or the fetish designs of the Utes and other Tribes. Floral designs are usually made with a size $10/^O$ or $11/^O$ beads, but with this kind of stitch the Shoshone and Arapahoe, among others, bead with the $13/^O$ Czech cut beads. In that a single thread holds many of the beads in place, for strength and durability, the strongest possible thread (or sinew) is used; "D" Nymo works well. As with other stitches explored, waxing is a must.

Bead graph paper is helpful in setting out designs, but in addition, in

(66A) c.1880 Man's Buckskin Vest, SIOUX. Fully beaded vest sewn with sinew in lazy stitch. (C)

(66B) c.1875 Pouch on Bandolier, JICARILLA APACHE Beaded with sinew on buckskin. (C)

(67A) c.1890 Buckskin Dress, SIOUX. Lazy stitched buckskin dress with leather fringe. Note the brass sequin adornment across bust and on lower sleeves. (E)

(68A) c.1870 Knife Case, BLACKFEET and (68B) c.1885 Knife Case, SIOUX. Both are made of rawhide. Notice the tin cones and brass nails as decorations on these fine examples. (E)

using overlaid stitches, the design is often mounted directly to the leather being beaded. On most Cree work the design is drawn on the reverse side in ball point pen. However, another method that offers some advantages can be used as follows: First, the design is drawn on paper; any paper of at least a medium weight will work, but brown "grocery sack" paper is used more than any other. Second, the design is "tacked" (sewn with one or two stitches in three or four places) to the leather. If the leather is very thin, or if it is material or canvas that is being beaded, one piece of paper may be tacked to the top and another to the bottom. This will help keep the beading material flat while the beading is being done (Do Not use glue). In either case, the paper with the design drawn on it is always tacked to the under side of the leather or material. This provides a pattern from which to bead, while at the same time it is possible to see the design take shape and make wanted corrections as the beading is done.

If a design is wanted that requires a "mirror image," such as on gloves, moccasins or leggin's, draw the design on a piece of paper. Then place this paper on top of another piece of paper and place these on top of a piece of carbon paper with the carbon up. Firmly trace over the drawn design on the top paper, and the opposed design will be on the bottom of the second paper. Carbon-made lines tend to be easily smeared and it is a good idea to retrace these lines with a pen. You can also insure that these lines will stay clear by spraying a small amount of hair spray over the finished pattern.

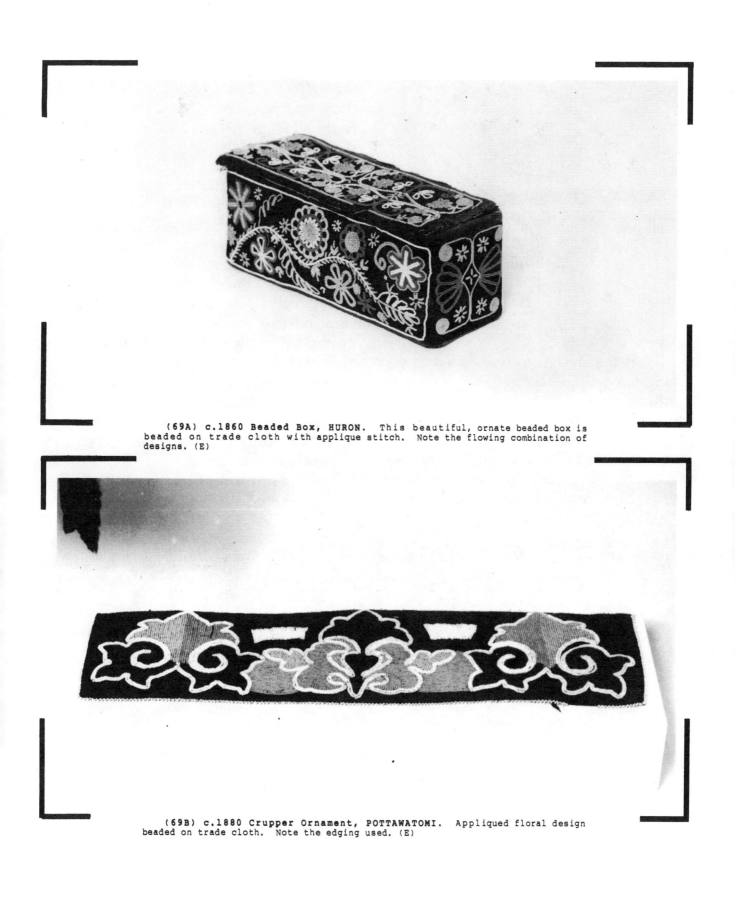

(69A) c.1860 Beaded Box, HURON. This beautiful, ornate beaded box is beaded on trade cloth with applique stitch. Note the flowing combination of designs. (E)

(69B) c.1880 Crupper Ornament, POTTAWATOMI. Appliqued floral design beaded on trade cloth. Note the edging used. (E)

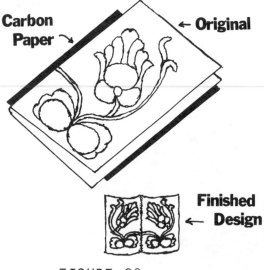

Carbon Paper ↘

← **Original**

Finished Design ←

FIGURE 22

If the design to be beaded is geometric, it will be useful to draw only the outline of the complete pattern on the back of the leather.

There are basically three variations of the overlaid stitch: The *Spot Stitch*, the *Running Stitch* and the *Return Stitch*. The variation used will depend on personal preference and on the requirements of the piece being beaded. **All of these methods produce a beaded look that is flat against the leather or material used**.

Both the spot and running stitches use two needles and threads. With the **spot stitch**, as shown below, after knotting one end of the thread it is brought through the leather and two or three beads are strung. These are laid next to the leather, and another needle and thread, also knotted, are brought up right next to the last bead. This thread goes over the thread with the beads on it and back into the leather. Another two or three beads are strung and this sequence is repeated. On extremely fine pieces or where sharp turns are necessary, only one bead will be strung and sewn down.

The **running stitch** is essentially the same except that enough beads are

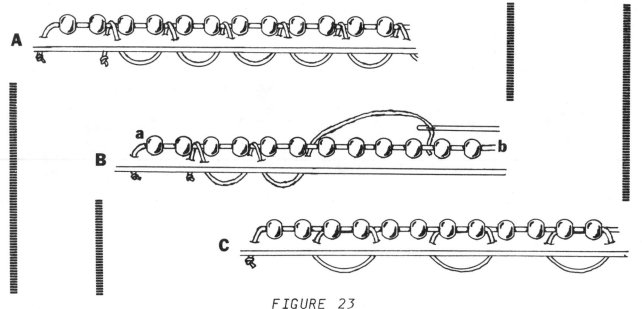

FIGURE 23
A - SPOT STITCH, B - RUNNING STITCH & C - RETURN STITCH

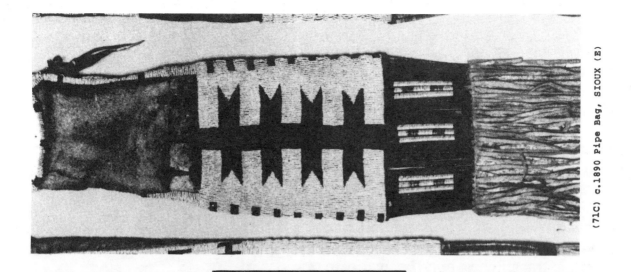

(71C) c.1890 Pipe Bag, SIOUX (E)

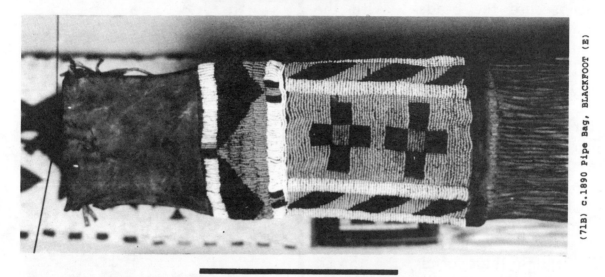

(71B) c.1890 Pipe Bag, BLACKFOOT (E)

(71A) c.1890 Pipe Bag, BLACKFOOT (E)

strung on the first thread to reach from point "A" to point "B" (see above) before it is taken back through the leather or material. Then the second thread is used to sew down the bead by going between every second or third bead. When beads are all of the same color, such as with geometric designs or floral background areas, it may be that only every fourth or fifth bead is sewn down. If, after a section is done, it does not look tight enough, extra stitches may be made to further secure the beads. With the running stitch it may be helpful to have the paper with the design drawn on it on top of the leather.

The **return stitch** uses only one needle and thread as shown. First knot the thread, and then bring it through the leather at the beginning of the design. String two or three beads and lay them next to the leather. The needle then goes down through the material next to the last bead and is brought back up next to the first bead. The needle is then taken back through these beads, the thread pulled tight, and two or three more beads are strung and the process repeated. It is possible when using this stitch to vary the number of beads that are strung. Also, if three beads are strung a tighter stitch can be made by coming back up between the last two, going through these, pulling the stitch tight and stringing three more beads. The advantage of this stitch over the other two methods is that only one needle is used and it is usually tighter when finished. However, it is also much slower.

(72A) c.1885 Tobacco Bag, CREE. Smoked buckskin bag with bead wrapped fringe and appliqued beaded pieces. Compare edge around bag with that around the beaded piece. (E)

(73C) c.1890 Pipe Bag, Cree (E)

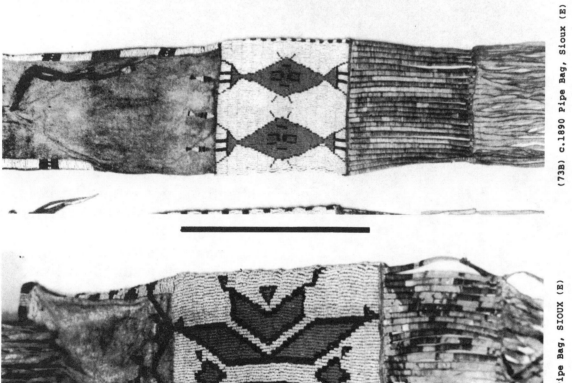

(73B) c.1890 Pipe Bag, Sioux (E)

(73A) c.1890 Pipe Bag, SIOUX (E)

When using any of these techniques it is probably a good idea in the beginning to use a shorter thread than with the lazy stitch. Also, with all of them, the outline of the design is beaded first and then the background is done. When the outline is completed the paper can be taken off of the leather. Remove the "tacks" that were made, and in most cases the paper will fall away from the beading because of the stitches that have been made through it. If it does not come off easily, use a sharp needle to remove it from around the beads. The background and filling in is now done using the same stitches.

SPACING

Two methods having to do with bead spacing will be helpful with any of these stitches. First, in the selection of beads, many areas will allow the use of the slightly larger or smaller beads that have been set aside from other stitches. In that floral designs have lines that curve, many times beads that are not uniform will fit just right. Second is a method called *crowding* or *spacing* of beads and this is extremely useful in backgrounds and with geometric designs. Simply put, this means either pulling beads extremely close together (crowding) or pulling them away from each other to fill more area (spacing). This is done by using the needle and thread to align the beads.

Crowding necessitates the most planning as you can only make the spaces

(75A) c.1875 Buckskin Shirt, **BLACKFEET.** Appliqued Buckskin shirt with
painted yoke. Note use of brass shoe buttons used to adorn center. (E)

(75B) c.1900 Bag, **BANNOCK.** Long lazy stitched buckskin bag trimmed with
trade cloth. Note the bead wrapping on the handle. (E)

between the beads smaller and not the beads themselves. Therefore, when it is found that the pattern will not align, it may be necessary to start pulling the beads closer together some five or six beads before the problem area. This is done by inserting the needle slightly behind the bead, going over the thread with the beads on it, taking the needle back through the leather at the same point and pulling the beads together tightly. With pre-planning, the beads should align properly.

Spacing is making the beads fit the design by leaving slightly larger spaces between them and is done by using the second needle and thread slightly in front of the bead being sewn into place. It is easy to see that the use of beads that are either larger or smaller than the rest is easier. This is not always possible, however, and these two techniques will be useful when needed.

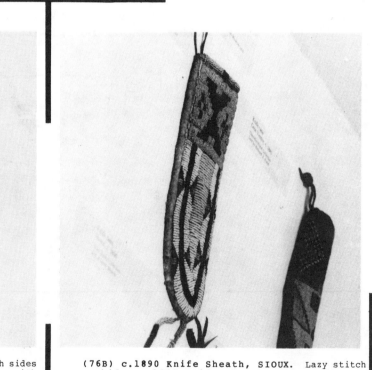

(76A) c.1875 Knife Sheath, SAC & FOX. Both sides shown, this is beaded over rawhide frame. Sewn with sinew (C)

(76B) c.1890 Knife Sheath, SIOUX. Lazy stitch on rawhide. c.1895 Knife Sheath, GROS VENTRE is visable above. (E)

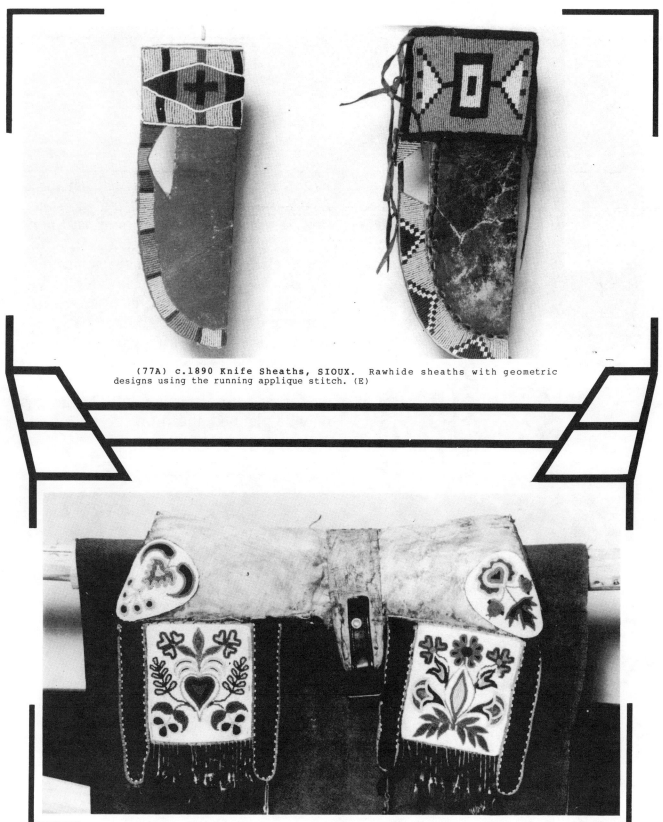

(77A) c.1890 Knife Sheaths, SIOUX. Rawhide sheaths with geometric designs using the running applique stitch. (E)

(77B) c.1885 Pad Saddle, CREE. Beautiful floral design saddle appliqued on buckskin with trade cloth trim. Note the glass crow bead tassles. (E)

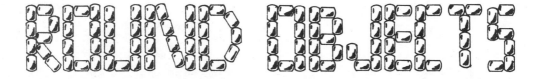

ROUND OBJECTS

There are two ways to bead round objects: **Bead Wrapping** and the **Peyote Stitch**. Bead wrapping is done by following the instructions given in the *Sewn Beadwork* section and using either the running or spot stitch. The only difference is that instead of using a flat pattern, the stitch is done around an object.

The peyote stitch is a bit more difficult, but develops into a very attractive finished item.

This stitch takes its name from the Peyote or Native American Church and is most often seen on gourd and fan handles, but as shown in the illustrations it may be used on any round or irregular shape such as salt and pepper shakers, canes, key chains, cigarette cases, earrings, bolo tie strings, etc. There are a number of things that make using this stitch easier: (1) uniform beads are absolutely necessary, (2) the object that is being beaded should be covered with felt or leather before starting and (3) patterns may be planned ahead on special "peyote graph paper" before beginning.

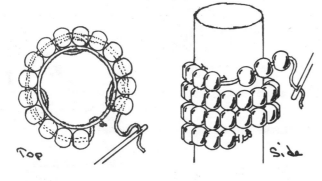

FIGURE 24 - BEAD WRAPPING

Bead Wrapping done by George "Two Hawk" Knowlden.

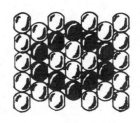

A

B

C

FIGURE 25

There are a number of variations of the peyote stitch, but *Figure 25* is a basic stitch that can be adapted to most round and irregular shaped items.

After the object has been covered with felt or leather, the first row of beads are secured to it leaving a very small space between each bead. The next row is then added as shown and so forth around the item. One use of this stitch that does not require securing the beading to an object is making earrings. In this case a drinking straw can be used as a base and after the earring is finished it is simply removed from the straw by sliding it off of it.

PEYOTE GRAPH PAPER

The following are some good examples of how Native Americans have used the Peyote Stitch of different items.

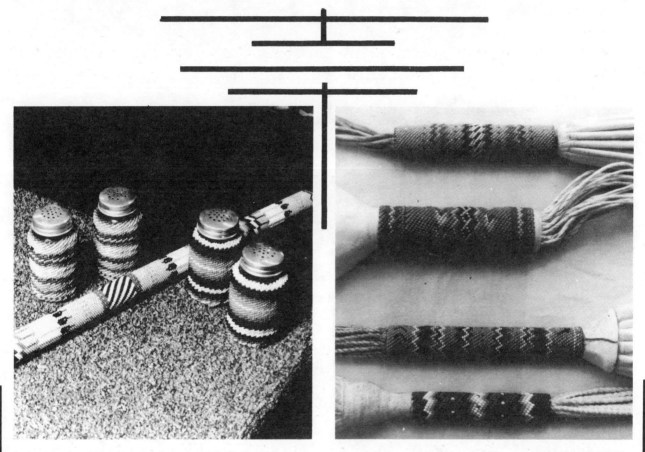

(79A) c.1980s Salt & Pepper Shakers and Cane, BANNOCK. Geometric designs done with peyote stitch. Note the intricate feather pattern on the cane. (F)

(79B) c.1970s Fan Handles, WINNEBAGO AND OMAHA. Designs are done in peyote stitch using 12/° and 13/° Czech cut beads. (A)

(80A) c.1980s Lighter Cases - round, SHOSHONE made by Mary Washakie, oval, KIOWA and Bottle Opener, BANNOCK. Contemporary peyote stitch (F).

(80B) c.1980s Fan Handle, BANNOCK. Made by Leonard Mosha with 12/° seed beads. (F)

(80C) c.1885 Crupper, CROW. Buckskin crupper done in "Crow Stitch." Note the hanging ornament made with brass hawk bells and wrapped beadwork. (E)

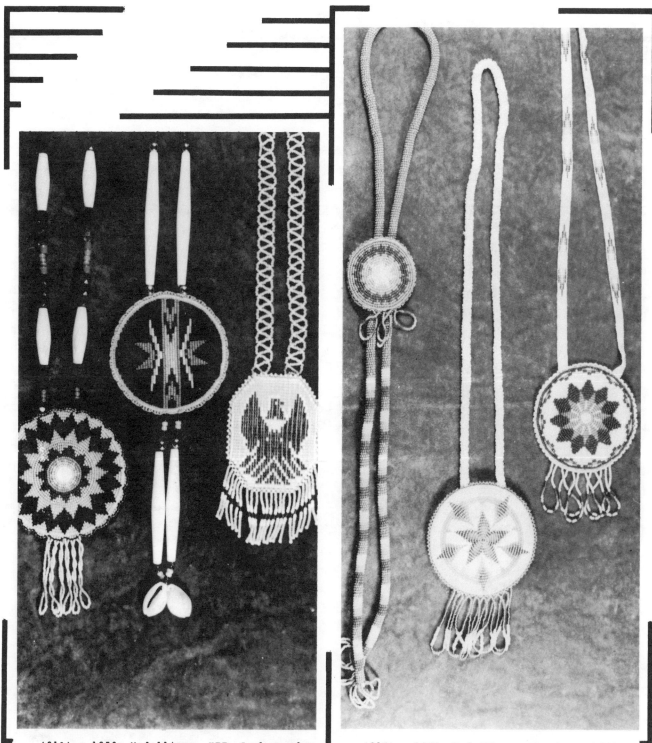

(81A) c.1950s Medallions, UTE. Good examples of the versatility of beaded medallions. From right to left these are rosette style, appliqued and loomed. Note the three different styles of edging. (B)

(81B) c.1950s Medallions, UTE. Nice medallions all done in rosette style. Notice the three different styles of necklaces. From left to right they are bead wrapping, daisy chain and loom work. (B)

81

eaded rosettes are very popular in contemporary craftwork and they provide an excellent item on which to practice the spot and running stitches described earlier in this book. Designs need to be studied and worked out in advance as the placement of beads is very important in doing a rosette. Uniform bead selection is necessary, but the use of beads that are slightly larger or smaller will also help in the alignment of designs.

Rosettes may be beaded to leather, felt or canvas but it is very important that the material used be absolutely flat during the beading. The "tacking" of medium weight paper (as described before) to the bottom and top of the material used will help keep it flat. Another method is to use embroidery hoops and, as the excess leather around the finished rosette will be cut away, this technique works well.

It is possible to start the beading from the outside and work in, or from the center and work out. As it is easier to gain a more uniform rosette, it is best for most beginning beadworkers to start in the center.

Begin by sewing down one bead in the center. Then, as with the running stitch, come out slightly more than 1/2 bead width, bring the needle up through the leather, and string enough beads to go around the center bead. The number of beads in this row will depend upon the size of the beads being used, and this will be the hardest row to get into place. After the beads are placed so that they **almost**, but not quite, touch the center bead, the second thread is used to sew them down. For this row it is best to sew between each bead. As each row is beaded in place

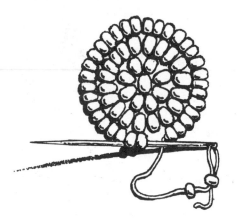

FIGURE 27

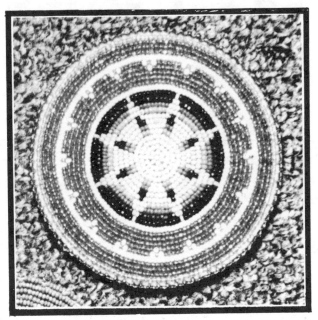

(82A) c.1980 Rosette, KIOWA. (F)

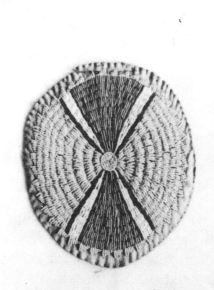

(83A) c.1978 Medallions, SIOUX. Beaded rosette style medallion. (A)

(83B) c.1875 Medallion, ARAPAHO. Traditional rosette beaded on buckskin with sinew. Middle is in rosette style and remained is made with lazy stitch. Size is 17.5 x 15 cm. in yellow and red.

(83C) c.1950s Medallions, UTE. Beaded in applique and rosette styles on buckskin. Note the daisy chain and 13/° cut beads on rectangle and three styles of edging shown. (B)

keep the leather flat and keep a tiny space between the rows. If the beads are made to touch, it will create a curved surface that is not wanted

The next rows can be sewn in place using either the running or spot stitch, but be careful to fit them in so that the design is made as desired. As noted above, the use of slightly different size beads will be useful in spots. As the next rows are made, it is not necessary to sew between each bead, but do it often enough (every two or three beads) to maintain a good flat, secure surface. When each circle or row is completed, run the needle and thread through the first two or three beads (as shown) before going back into the leather so that a space is not left.

When the rosette is completed it should lie perfectly flat. If it does not, it usually means that the thread has been pulled too tightly, and that forces the beads together. As with all beading, it requires practice and patience to produce award winning work. Do not give up as excellent beadwork can be produced in a surprisingly short time.

Again, if the material that the rosette has been beaded on to is to be mounted on leather, be sure to use needle and thread to do this. If any glue at all is used, a couple of spots to hold the two pieces together while sewing will be enough.

For the last step in making rosettes and many beaded pieces, see the chapter on Edging.

(84A) c.1955 Coin Purse, UTE. Beautiful rosette style appliqued purse beaded on buckskin from the Ms. Bessie Wardle Collection. (B)

(84B) c.1980 Rosettes, SHOSHONI. Assorted patterns of beaded rosettes. Note the use of different kinds of beads for affect. (F)

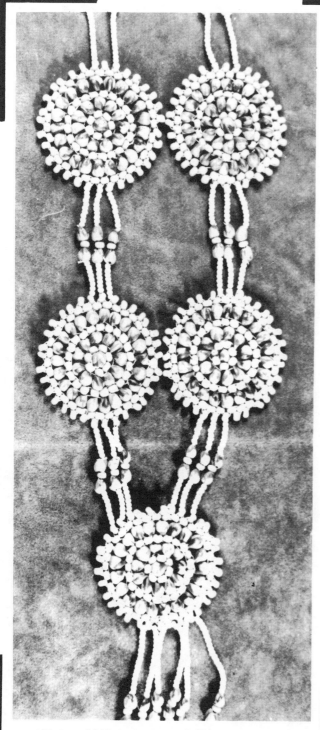

(85A) c.1920 Rosette Medallion, NAVAJO. Good example of rosette work with pony and ghost beads with 10/° seed beads in necklace. (B)

(85B) c.1950s Necklace and Bolo Tie, UTE. Rosette style appliqued necklace with peyote stitch beaded cords. Note edging on medallions. (B)

85

BEADED NECKLACES

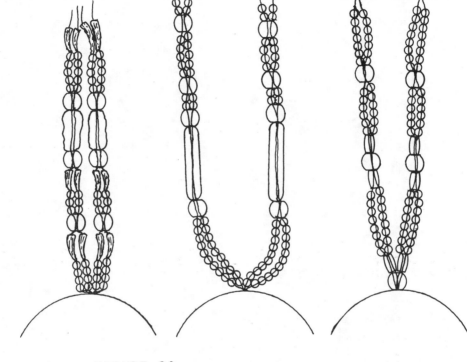

FIGURE 28

The stringing of beads of various types has been an Indian vocation from pre-history and many Tribes wear many strung beads in their ceremonials. Shown here are a few that are suggested in Preston Miller's book (see *Selected Bibliography*). The examples above would serve well for holding rosettes, but are a small sample of what is possible in making necklaces. Materials that can be used include dentalium shell, crow beads, pony beads, seed beads, bone hairpipe and tubes, trade beads, bugle beads of various sizes or even 15/º hexigon beads.

In that the necklaces have to support weight and are subject to wear, a size "F" thread works well. This necessitates a size 10 needle and limits the kinds of beads that may be used.

Stringing needles are often available at craft supply houses and can save time in stringing. These needles are made of wire and are generally 4 to 6 inches in length. With these needles it is possible to use imitation sinew to good effect in stringing.

In any case, be sure and match the

needle and thread to the kinds of beads
that are being used.

DAISY CHAINS

Another popular method of mak-
ing necklaces or beaded strings is to make
a *Daisy Chain*. Two techniques are dia-
grammed on the right and either of these
makes up into an attractive necklace.

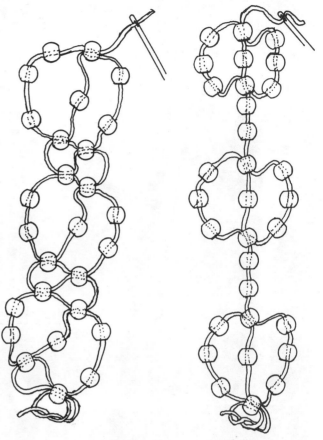

FIGURE 29

(87A) c.1970s Bead Necklace, **WINNEBAGO.** Photo
of Mrs. Maggie Smith in traditional Winnebago ribbon
work blouse and skirt with necklace of strung bugle
beads. Mrs. Smith continues to produce outstanding,
realistic dolls. (A)

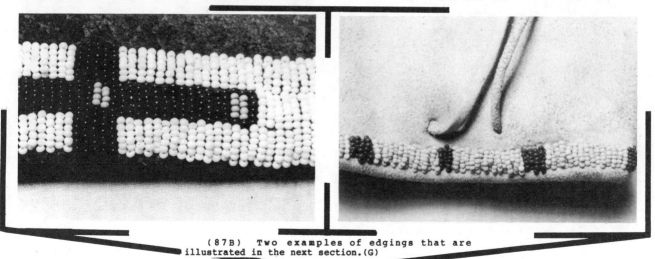

(87B) Two examples of edgings that are
illustrated in the next section.(G)

(88A) c.1870 War Shirt, CROW. Modified lazy stitch war shirt with horse hair and ermine tails adornment. Note the complimentary beaded patterns. (E)

EDGINGS

The different kinds of edging are almost limitless and the examples given here are but a very few of the many that are possible to use. In almost all of the edging that is done, however, it is a good idea to use both threads on the needle as there is a lot of wear on this exposed part of beading, and strength and durability is needed. Therefore, when the knot is made, make it with both ends of the thread after the needle has been strung.

Although most edging is done for decorative reasons, often it will be used as a means to attach a lining or backing to the beadwork.

All of the examples given below (*Figures A* thru *M*), are completed as the last step of the beading project.

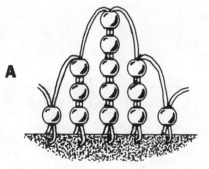

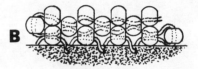

Left (90A) c.1920 Shirt, **NORTHERN PLAINS.** Contemporary style open front jacket with short fringe. Note the elaborate beaded figurines and geometric design trim. Right (90B) c.1890 Shirt, **NORTHERN PLAINS.** Note the unusual geometric designs all done in lazy stitch technique. (E)

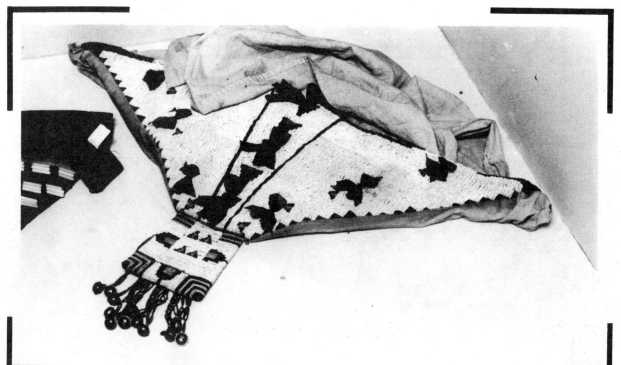

(91A) c.1895 Cradle Board Cover, ARAPAHO. Simple designed lazy stitched piece with ribbon and brass hawk bells for decoration. (E)

E

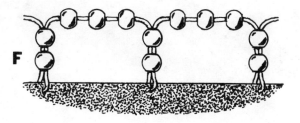

F

G

H

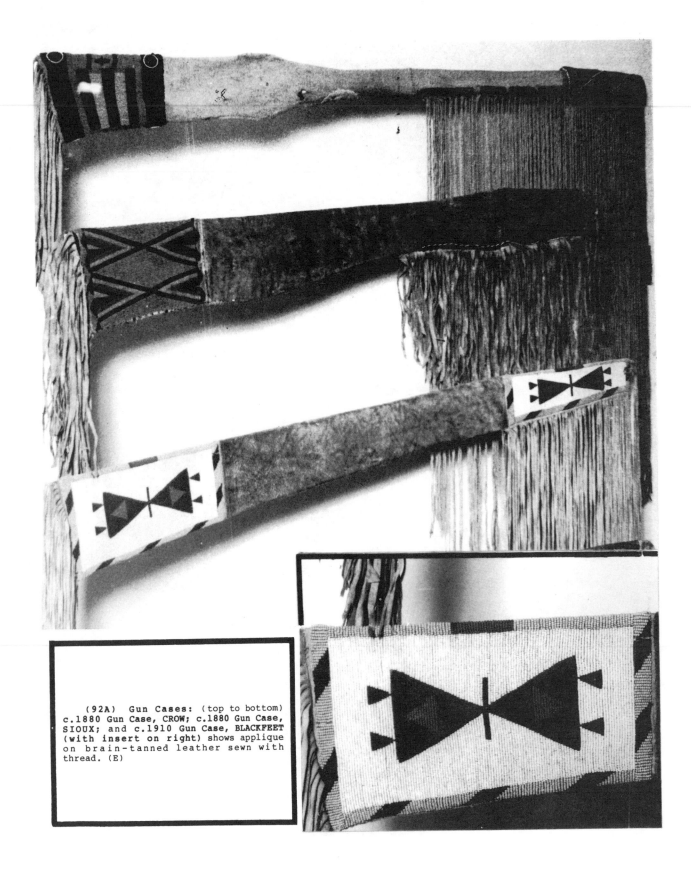

(92A) Gun Cases: (top to bottom)
c.1880 Gun Case, CROW; c.1880 Gun Case,
SIOUX; and c.1910 Gun Case, BLACKFEET
(with insert on right) shows applique
on brain-tanned leather sewn with
thread. (E)

J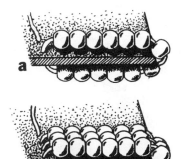

a

b

K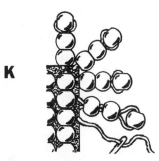

L

M

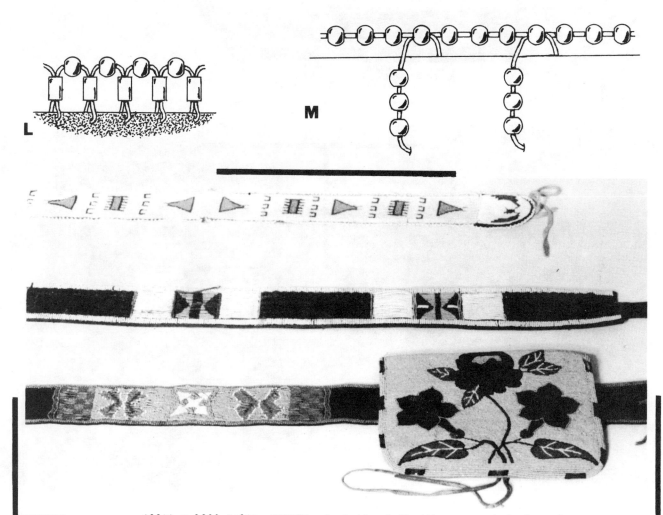

(93A) c.1900 Belts, YAKIMA. On bottom belt with purse, note horizontal
lazy stitch with applique technique on purse design. (E)

(94A) c.1880 Storage Bag, BLACKFEET. Fully applique beaded bag done on brain-tanned buckskin. (E)

(94B) c.1875 Pouch, MOHAWK. 18 x 17.5 cm. velveteen U-shaped pouch with flaps front and back. Edge bound with red cloth and 10/° seed beads. (C)

(94C) c.1890 Breechcloth, POTAWATOMI. Very nice applique work on black cloth. Maltese cross design with floral pattern. Edged with purple satin ribbon. (C)

The following "NOTES" are not necessary for doing beadwork, but might be of interest to the general reader:

<<<<< INTRODUCTION >>>>>

(1) Two of Orchard's works that are in print and should be read by anyone interested in the craftwork of the North American Indian are **The Techniques of Porcupine Quill Decoration Among the Indians of North America** and **Beads and Beadwork of the American Indian**. The quote in the Foreward is from page 167 of the last book noted above.

(2) I find it interesting that men have produced most of the best books on beadwork. In addition to the Orchard books noted above there are **Crow Indian Beadwork** by Wildschut & Ewers, **Craft Manual of Northwest Indian Beading** by George White, **Four Winds Indian Beadwork and Old Flathead Photos**, by Preston Miller, **American Indian Beadwork** by Hunt & Burshears and **Beads: Thier Use by Upper Great Lakes Indians** edited by Gordon Olson.

An exception to this male oriented enterprise is **Quill and Beadwork of the Western Sioux** by Carrie A. Lyford. The B.I.A. orientation of this book makes it difficult to read, but it does contain some good information on dates and patterns.

<<< GENERAL INFORMATION >>>

(1) There are a number of good books on the history of beads and their usage. Many of these can be found in the following Selected Bibliography but a couple of books that are directed to the general reader are Orchard's **Beads and Beadwork . . .** (Pgs 15-150) and **Beads: Their Use By Upper Great Lakes Indians** (Pgs 2-33).

(2) On the various dates that beads were introduced to Tribes by the Fur Traders, it is interesting to compare Lyford's dates for the Sioux with Wildschut's for the Crow.

(3) Dates and information in this section come from books noted in the Selected Bibliography Section. The use of seed beads as early as 1500 AD comes from the well researched Nesbitt paper.

(4) A statistic almost as useful as "One hank of 10/° beads will cover about 12 square inches . . ." is that on a 20" string you will get approximately 295 10/° beads, 340 11/° beads, 370 12/° beads, 415 13/° beads and 465 14/° beads.

(5) Many times an authentic looking reproduction is easier to make using Italian beads.

(6) Japanese 15/° Hexigon beads have gained alot of popularity at this writing. They may be used in place of 13/° Czech Cut Beads and tend to be uniform. Because of the edges, the thread must be waxed.

(96A) c.1900 Shirt, PIEGAN BLACKFOOT. Lazy stitch beaded vest on brain-tanned buckskin. (E)

(96B) c.1915 Vest, FLATHEAD. Beaded vest on buckskin with white seed bead background and design in 13/° Czech cut beads. Adorned with glass facetted beads and cowry shells. (E)

<<<<< DESIGNS >>>>>

(1) Anyone interested in quillwork should see the Orchard book on Quill Decoration. This book is still the definitive work on porcupine quillwork and most of the techniques are shown.

(2) Much of contemporary quillwork is done with nymo thread, but there are still many craftspersons who use sinew.

(3) The floral designs of the Northern Woodland Tribes reflect the influence of the French Catholic Nuns. Craftwork done before that period show alot of geometric inclinations.

(4) For an outstanding book on authentic craftwork, see **Hau, Kola** from the Plains Indian Collection of the Haffenreffer Museum of Anthropology. The book is also an excellent source of design patterns.

(5) On the "test" of tribal significance of designs: An empirical study of same was conducted on the Santee Sioux Reservation in 1978. Twenty-five elders were contacted and the results were as reported in the text. There was no indication of Tribal significance whatsoever.

(6) A notable use of beads for inter-tribal communication was the belts of waumpum. In this case, color seemed to be the "shared communicator," and designs were a kind of short-hand.

(7) The quote from Robert Lowie is from **Crow Indian Bead-work**, Page 47.

<<<<< LOOMWORK >>>>>

(1) The "bow loom" was constructed using a bent tree limb and was fairly common to the Woodland Tribes. It was very difficult to use and fragil; the loom offers no advantages over the looms shown in the text.

SELECTED BIBLIOGRAPHY

Books that are marked with an (+) are "how to do" beadwork text that are currently available.

Bowdoin Gil, Carl A., **Native North American Seedbeading Techniques**, The Bead Journal, vol. III, No. 2, 1977.

Densmore, Frances. **Chippewa Customs**, Forty-fourth Annual Report of the Bureau of American Ethnology, Washington, D.C., 1929.

Denver Art Museum, **Leaflets**, No. 2. "North American Plains Indians Hide Dressing and Bead Sewing Techniques," 1930. No. 117. "Beadwork History and Technics," 1953. Nos. 118-119, "Main Types of Sewn Beadwork," 1953

Grand Rapids Public Museum, **Beads: Thier Use By Upper Great Lakes Indians**, Grand Rapids, 1977.

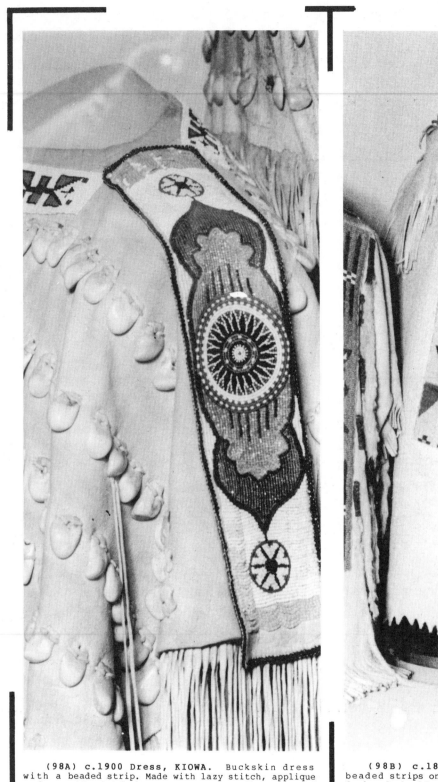

(98A) c.1900 Dress, KIOWA. Buckskin dress with a beaded strip. Made with lazy stitch, applique and rosette techniques. Dress has elk teeth tied with buckskin thongs. (E)

(98B) c.1890 Shirt, BLACKFEET. Appliqued beaded strips on buckskin shirt. Note the different designed shoulder beadstrip. (E)

Gringhuis, Dirk. "Indian Costume at Mackinac: Seventeenth and Eighteenth Century," **Mackinac History**, vol. II, No. 1, Lansing, 1972

Haffenreffer Museum of Anthropology, **Hau, Kola!**, Providence, 1982.

Hunt, Ben & Burshears, "Buck", **American Indian Beadwork**, New York, 1983 (+).

Jacobs, Wilbur R., **Wilderness Politics and Indian Gifts: The Northern Colonial Frontier 1748-1763**, Lincoln, 1966.

Johnson, Judi, "American Indian Beadwork," **The Explorer**, vol 18, No. 4, 1976

Karklins, Karlis, and Sprague, Roderick, "Glass Trade Beads in North America: An Annotated Bibliography, **Historical Archeology**, 1972.

Lyford, Carrie A., **Quill and Beadwork of the Western Sioux**, Boulder, 1982 (+).

Miller, Preston, **Four Winds Indian Beadwork and Old Flathead Photos**, St. Ignatius, 1972 (+).

Nesbitt, Alexander, "Glass," **South Kensington Museum Art Handbook**, London, 1878.

Norton, Thomas E., **The Fur Orade in Colonial New York 1686-1776**, Madison, 1974.

Orchard, William C., **Beads and Beadwork of the American Indian**, New York, 1929 (+)

Orchard, William C., **The Technique of Porcupine Quill Decoration Among the Indians of North America**, Eagle's View Publishing, Ogden, Utah, 1982.

Pratt, Peter P., **Oneida Iroquois Glass Trade Bead Sequence 1595-1745**, Syracuse, 1961.

Quimby, George I., **Indian Culture and European Trade Goods**, Madison, 1966.

Quimby, George I., **Indian Life in the Upper Great Lakes: 11,000 B.C. to A.D. 1800** , Chicago, 1960.

White, George M., **Craft Manual of Northwest Indian Beading**, Ronan, 1982 (+).

Wildschut, William & Ewers, John C. **Crow Indian Beadwork**, New York, 1978 (+)

Woodward, Arthur, **The Denominators of the Fur Trade: An Anthology of Writings on the Material Culture of the Fur Trade**, Pasadena, 1970.

Woodward, Arthur, **Indian Trade Goods**, Portland, 1965.

(100A) c.1945 Necktie, UTE. Appliqued floral design beaded necktie and collar. These were fairly common on the Ute Reservation during the early reservation period. Note edging. (B)

(100B) c.1950s Purse, UTE. Fully beaded purse with zippered front and peyote stitched strap. Note the use of bead colors to create assortment of shading effects in design. (B)

INDEX